Conversations in Communication ®

Volume II

Customer Relationship Management (CRM) as a Function of Public Relations

—ɯ—

by
Jabaree Dunham-Carson

edited by
Philip Weinholtz

Customer Relationship Management (CRM) as a Function of
Public Relations

Customer Relationship Management (CRM) as a Function of
Public Relations

Conversations in Communication® Volume II

Customer Relationship Management (CRM) as a Function of
Public Relations

Copyright © 2015 by Jabaree Dunham-Carson

Cover Illustration by: Lee Woodgate
http://www.leewoodgate.com/

ISBN-10: 0-9960033-4-7
ISBN-13: 978-0-9960033-4-6

Customer Relationship Management (CRM) as a Function of
Public Relations

Foreword

Despite the economic downturn of 2009, businesses are booming once again. Along with this growth is an unprecedented volume of business intelligence and data.

In Conversations in Communication, Volume II, Jabaree Dunham-Carson explores the current state of CRM tools and how they shape business interactions. By exploring a variety of software options and users' perceptions of organizations, Dunham offers a succinct and accurate portrayal of how companies can grow and thrive with the use of contemporary CRM software.

This text allows us to grow our understanding of CRM systems and how they define the future of business in the technology era.

Philip Weinholtz
Founder, Full Media Services LLC

Customer Relationship Management (CRM) as a Function of
Public Relations

The purpose of this study was to discover if Customer Relationship Management (CRM) programs could serve as a function of Public Relations in the development of stakeholder relationships. Traditionally associated with marketing and sales, CRM has reinvented the ways an organization is able to satisfy issues concerning customers by strengthening a customer's association with an organization (Reimann, Schilke, & Thomas, 2010). As CRM continues to grow among organizational professionals, the links between marketing, retention, loyalty, and customer satisfaction have become the driving forces behind implementation. In contrast, there are many who question the purpose of CRM programming, due to a range of vague definitions and consistently redefined expectations. In an attempt to break away from the traditional assumptions of public relations professionals, new strategic business plans emphasize improving customer rapport by supporting the needs of the customer, as well as analyzing how a company responses to a given situation.

A study was conducted to analyze CRM communication by exploring the organization-public (OP) relationships between customers and their banking providers. Surveys were distributed using a snowball-convenience sample throughout the northeast region of the United States, with the majority of surveys administered to students, staff, faculty, and associates of The University of Hartford. The goal of the survey was to generate customer perspectives regarding an organization's reputation, communication, and overall banking experience. The responses were also analyzed to see if organizations could improve customer loyalty, identification, retention, and overall satisfaction via CRM communication. The results from this study provided strong correlations between satisfaction, reputation, goodwill, and identification, offering new insight on the connection between CRM, Public Relations, and customer association.

Table of Contents

Introduction:

The growth and success of an organization depends not only upon the product or service offered, but how effectively the organization can develop a relationship with consumers and sustain their relationship with current customers. Whether the customer is an unknown individual within a random demographic, targeted by market research, or has continuously sustained a relationship with the organization for several years, a business must continue to appear innovative, credible, and available to meet the needs of potential consumers. Several scholars in the fields of communication, public relations, and marketing, acknowledge the importance of customer recognition and support the premise of organizational management, specifically for relationship building and providing customers with external resources (Mithas, Krishnan, & Fornell, 2005). The process of customer retention comes from an organization's investment in data collection, their use of theories to explain customer/consumer behavior, and acknowledging communicative concepts that encourage new methods to sustain relationships between population segments. This is initiated via Customer Relationship Management (CRM[1]), a relational method used by organizations to gather information through an extensive analysis of consumer behavior, in addition to facilitating communication by way of providing customer touch points (Mithas et al, 2005).

While the concepts and tools employed for CRM processing will vary among companies, the expansive set of programs and applications each work toward increasing

---

[1] A list of all acronyms used can be found in Appendix A

the rapport among business-to-business (B2B) or business-to-consumer (B2C) relationships. The intention of CRM programs is to attain customer insights, beliefs, attitudes, and perspectives (Mithas et al, 2005) so that the company in return can attempt to meet the demands of their stakeholders while retaining their customer base. CRM functions are also instituted to encourage customer usage of a service, product, or establishment, along with preserving customers who currently use services provided from an organization (Aurier & N'Goala, 2010). As the multitude of CRM instruments increase, the opportunities for customers to connect with an organization will undoubtedly increase a company's ability to discover new consumer populations while simultaneously maintaining customer retention rates.

The possibilities of CRM are further discussed by Aurier and N'Goala (2010), suggesting that program functions heavily emphasize the customer in order to retrieve individual levels of customer loyalty, customer rates of product consumption, and to increase each customer's level of profit contribution to a company. CRM's ability to support both customer and profit growth also assists program intentions to reduce the loss of clients to other businesses by sustaining open channels of communication between businesses and consumers. When customers are familiar with an organization, they have the ability to make implicit decisions of consumption, due to their previous purchasing experiences and innate knowledge of what is offered (Musalem & Joshi, 2009). Knowledge of customer preferences can lead to effective marketing campaigns (Musalem & Joshi, 2009) and when relationships are achieved, individual customer attention can be provided to consumers. This in return, produces a cycle of knowledge between marketing, relationship management (via CRM) and profitability from consumption.

In spite of the principle foundations positioned under CRM, there are many in both the professional world and academia who denounce the profitability and overall effectiveness of CRM program modules that claim to improve consumer relationships. Several scholars question the validity of studies that initially give praises to CRM functions, yet are vague in how CRM functions actually influence customer satisfaction (Mithas et al, 2005). Critiques from companies that have applied CRM programs claim that only 25-30% of their organizations felt as though they invested into a functional processing system, while other companies have suggested that the customer themselves should be in control of maintaining connections to the organization (Mithas et al, 2005). In addition to concerns of efficiency, businesses with CRM investments are reported to have issues relating to the implementation process, the ease of usage from customers who evaluate the programs, and have become indifferent to paying for CRM products that may only produce limited empirical evidence to support an increase in customer satisfaction (IEE Solutions, 2002).

With professionals and scholars debating upon the actual impressions left from CRM programs upon customer satisfaction and customer retention, there is little research that theoretically connects an individual's social environment as a reason to establish a relationship between an organization and its customers. This topic of environmental influence is worthy of further investigation because of our societal connections between perception, attitudes, and collective influence. When an individual is driven by internal attitudes, he or she may alter their perspective based on how others around them may feel about their association with a product or an organization (Ajzen, 1991).

The goal of this research is to discover if Customer Relationship Management programs can function as a mediator for Public Relations in the development of stakeholder relationships. Knowing this information, a company may have the ability to revitalize customer relationships and approach their consumer population from an alternative perspective. If an organization capitalizes upon their public relationships with consumers by researching the societal reputation and credibility of the company, the strength of their Organization-Public (OP) relationships can lead to significant strides in the amount of data that would be collected using CRM programs. Organizations would have the ability to track the individual's attitudes and levels of satisfaction, and use them as an indicator of public endorsement regarding the company, in addition to improving their relationship management tactics.

Chapter I

Purpose for CRM Development

The driving success behind any organization is the ability to develop, establish, and sustain a profitable relationship with clients and consumers. A company's decision to maximize customer satisfaction as an operational priority has only recently received the terminology and programming identification by way of 'Customer Relationship Management' (Aurier & N'Goala, 2010). Continuously redefined by scholars, marketers, and salespersons, some consider the primary application of CRM functionality is to support business sales strategies in order to increase profitability and performance (Reimann, Schilke, & Thomas, 2010). Additional scholars emphasize managerial influence is need when attempting to utilize CRM programs, as they are able to oversee the opportunities generated to improve customer satisfaction with an organization (Reimann et al, 2010). CRM tactics not only support financial growth, but also give recognition to the individual equity values that each customer brings to the organization through association (Aurier & N'Goala, 2010).

There are, however, many who refute the ideology of CRM and question its true purpose within an organization. A number of researchers have reviewed CRM programs, only to be left puzzled and frustrated with claims of strategies and theories that provide limited evidence of actual benefit to organizational performance (Reimann et al, 2010). Speier and Venkatesh (2002) found that numerous organizations fail at successful implementation because of an ill-defined set of expectations that are associated with CRM, and companies eventually disengage from their association with CRM modules. Despite the conflict of definition, the generalized expectation of CRM is that a company, when applying CRM programming and tactics, can encourage customer involvement and proliferate communication through involvement.

Traditionally associated with marketing and sales, CRM has reinvented the ways an organization is able to satisfy issues concerning consumers by strengthening a customer's association with an organization (Reimann et al, 2010). As a sales tool, CRM presence emerged throughout the 1990's in business magazines as a component that managed customer input of the demographic information collected from segmented consumers to increase profitability and customer loyalty (Kale, 2005). Sales and marketing departments were able to use CRM tools as accessories to solidify contracts and continue contact with customers by using sales force automation (SFA) tools to make phone calls, send messages, and collect data (Speier & Venkatesh, 2002). Over the years, the responsibility of CRM has expanded to all divisions of a company that have any form of contact with potential consumers. CRM supported departments can include, but are not limited to, marketing, sales, human resources, information technologies (IT), product supply management, corporate communications, and public relation departments (Kale, 2005; Speier & Venkatesh, 2002). Successful businesses collectively contribute to customer maintenance and assist customers with their concerns and inquiries by ensuring that all departments are knowledgeable in CRM functions.

It goes without question that the impact of relationship development between businesses and their customer base is the principle foundation of CRM. Chao, Chu and Lee (2011) discuss the benefits of an organization's investment in customer development, which can result in elevated levels of comfort and trust, decreased feelings of organizational uncertainly of services offered, and increased organization credibility. More organizations continue to recognize the need to finance customer relationships, as the companies who rely upon communication with their stakeholders recognize the influence customers have upon price formation and product distribution, ultimately effecting brand recognition (Ramaseshan et al. 2006; Reimann et al, 2010).

Relationship Development

In the past, elements of traditional marketing were a simple, a one-way process of communication, with an organization providing the public with advertisements, salespersons, and the guarantee that there product was trustworthy, reliable, and effective (Jayachandran, Sharma, Kaufman & Raman, 2005). Today our expectations as consumers have skyrocketed to include multiple points of interaction with organizations that expand over several media platforms. Every possible avenue of communication can now be used by organizations to sustain contact with all members of the public, creating the ideal relationship between the producer and consumer. Jayachandran et al, (2005) provide extensive detail of the benefits surrounding organization-customer relationships in their study discussing the role of relational information within CRM. When customers invest into a product or service, if that relationship is acknowledged and supported by the company, the organization receives higher evaluations for positive perceptions, as well as gains in overall customer share (CS) (Jayachandran, et al, 2005). The CS value is computed as the ratio of customer purchases of a select product from one company within a category, compared to a customer's total number purchases of the same product from all possible competitors within the same category (Peppers and Rogers, 1999, as cited by Jayachandran et al, 2005). Increases in CS value are vital to an organization's market share and profitability due to the information it provides in determining whether an organization's marketing tactics were effective, as well as data supporting organizational perceptions and brand influence.

Studies from Aurier and N'Goala (2010) also note the importance of CRM upon relationship development and maintenance, which leads to extended customer life value (CLV) rates from committed individuals. Their evaluation of trust and commitment as essential elements of relationship management go beyond the initial contact with consumers, suggesting that the best formed customer relationships are those that provide cognitive feelings of support, identification and affiliation between the organization and the customer:

> "Therefore, while trust is based on an evaluation of the partner's qualities (perceived reliability and integrity); relationship commitment involves a psychological attachment, a concern for the welfare of the organization. In this affective approach, relationship commitment results more from an identification process (congruence in values, affiliation and belongingness) than from an evaluation process where it is worth maintaining the current exchange relationship" (Aurier & N'Goala, 2010, p.307).

As trust builds among customers, so does the ability to increase satisfaction, expectations, and approval, which in

return creates patterns for customer retention. When
companies use CRM tools to facilitate evaluations of
products, and of the organization overall, a level of
assurance in privacy and credibility must be present for
consumers who voluntarily provide personal details of
intimate information. When a customer grows to a point of
identification with a company (such as being a proud
owner of "product A"), their relational confidence in their
CRM involvement increases, as well as their potential to
continuously invest into the organization (Aurier &
N'Goala, 2010).

Customer Satisfaction

CRM relationships have the ability to collect all forms
of personal information, providing an organization the
opportunity to increase satisfaction among customers by
creating a familiar environment, limiting the need for a
customer to terminate their affiliation (Chao et al, 2011).
When a relationship has lasted for an extended period, it is
usually due to the organization taking the initiative in
learning more about customer needs, rather than simply
telling the customer what is best for them. Long-term
customers consistently associate with the same
organizations because they are familiar with the
organization's stance on customer preference. Customer
who have greater knowledge of products or services
offered will recall their commitment and investment to the
organization, reducing their levels of anxiety that come
from situations of uncertainty (Bell, Auh, & Smalley,
2005).   In addition to levels of comfort, the best
organizations recognize that every relationship is mutually
exclusive, resulting in the need to meet the needs of each
individual relationship in order to remain successful (Bell,
Auh, & Smalley, 2005).

When considering the applicability of relationship development and CRM processes, a basic theory regarding profit from customers is the 80/20 rule. Chao et al (2011) elaborate on the basic belief behind the premise of 80/20, suggesting that 80% of profit from an organization will be generated from 20% of the customers. As Chao et al (2011) reviewed the natural connections between customer development and CRM who predicted that if businesses increased their number of customers by 5%, the opportunity to raise profits will be within the range of 25%-85%, depending upon the environment of the industry to which the organization operates (Reichheld & Sasser, 1990). Chao et al (2011), continues to reinforce the value of customer-organizational relationships, submitting the argument that, with this logic, a simple 2% retention rate of customers for an organization can lead to a 10% savings in marketing methods for obtaining new customers.

As CRM continues its aggregation among marketing and organizational professionals, the link between marketing, retention, loyalty, and customer satisfaction continues to be the driving force behind implementation. Recognizing the profitability of the consuming public, organizations can use customer information to determine exclusive methods to increase CRM's return on investment (ROI) through unique approaches to marketing and customer service (Blattberg et al. 2001; Reinartz et al. 2004; Thomas et al.2004; Reimann et al, 2010). By assuring the customer that they are *the* substantial contribution to the success of an organization, a company provides the customer with the belief that they are not simply a number, and in return the consumer manifests a sense of recognition and identification. However, the methods that marketers, salespersons, PR practitioners, and human resource departments use to capitalize upon CRM programs and data will vary by the size of a department. The amount of funding allocated to CRM production, and the amount of support given to the various CRM tools from upper management and the dominant coalition is also an important factor that has a large role in effective implementation.

**Conversations in Communication ®
Volume II**

Customer Relationship Management (CRM) as a Function of Public Relations

1. Only 25-30% of investors are confident of their knowledge/understanding of the CRM investment

25-30%

2. Failure rates of CRM programs/projects have reached as high as 70% due to failed implementation

70%

"Critiques from companies that have applied CRM programs claim that only 25-30% of their organizations felt as though they invested into a functional processing system…. (Mithas et al. 2005)….Reimann et al (2010) highlight the failure rates of CRM projects to be as high as 70%, either producing losses for a company or no substantial improvement (The Gartner Group. 2003)." -

Jabaree Dunham-Carson

Innovations to Customer Rapport

Any situation that involves direct communication between an organization and members of the public has the ability to be analyzed and critiqued from the perspective of a public relations (PR) practitioner. The various associations that develop between a company, their active consumers, extended stakeholders, and the general population, each have a significant bearing upon

relational development, affecting an organization's ability
to increase financial growth, customer base, positive public
perceptions, and product evaluations (Bruning, 2001).
Relationship Management (RM) is the quintessential
foundation of a successful relationship that forms between
businesses and consumers. Recent studies in
organizational communication have led to a reevaluation
of the roles and beliefs associated with a PR practitioner.
Bruning (2001) discusses the transformation of the PR
professional, who initially centered upon media
representation and supported organizational publicity
(Cardwell, 1997), but is now garnished with a new
emphasis toward interactive, supervisory responsibilities.
RM creates a new set of tasks within public relations,
encouraging organizations and their practitioners to
develop well-rounded managerial skills in order to
increase the rate of positive organization-public (OP)
relationships among consumers (Bruning, 2001).

In an attempt to break away from the traditional
obligations assumed of public relations professionals, new
strategic business plans among organizations now
anticipate and emphasize the importance of improving
customer rapport, supporting the needs of the customer,
and analyzing how a company responses to a given
situation. PR practitioners are increasingly aware of how
impactful CRM is upon meeting stakeholder expectations
and prompting societal reputations, resulting in RM's
placement as an upper-level priority among the
organizational issues dealt with by the dominant coalition
(Hong & Yang, 2009). Determining ways to manage
customers, relationships, and societal obligations are
challenges that many organizations struggle with, often
invoking unsettled presumptions from stakeholders, and

action from members of the public (Reinartz, Krafft, &
Hoyer, 2004).

It is when a company decides to invest into PR
strategies and tactics that relationships foster among
stakeholders, allowing the PR practitioner to develop and
assist the process of increasing levels of customer
satisfaction (Bruning & Ledingham, 1998). Ledingham's
(2003) PR research on relationship management from a
'relational perspective' focuses on multiple frameworks PR
practitioners must consider when formulating strategies
and tactics to communicate with publics. While the theory
is well rounded, covering multiple aspects of PR
population identification, CRM and Corporate Social
Responsibility (CSR) tactics, when managed properly
under the umbrella of Ledingham's relational perspective
of RM, each contribute essential relational functions for
OP relationship development, customer retention and
consumer satisfaction. Understanding the effectiveness
of communication between organizations and publics can
lead to increased customer knowledge and overall
retention (Horn, Feinberg, & Salvendy, 2005). CRM and
CSR embedded within RM also assists PR practitioners in
discovering new methods to improve public perceptions,
increase market influence and market share, and allow for
projections of future customer and financial growth
through the social contributions provided from the
organization (Luo & Bhattacharya, 2006).

Chapter II

Public Relations
Definition and background.

To fully appreciate how CRM and CSR strategies enhance RM communication between organizations, stakeholders, and the public, one must understand how vital relationship building is in fortifying the foundation of public relations. Bruning (2001) recaps the history of PR, which during its early stages had several organizational duties, ranging from media relations, publicity, advertising, and information gathering among publics and employees (as cited by Cardwell, 1997). Continuously subjected to reevaluations, PR has since shifted from journalistic principles (Gronstedt, 1997) to a more consistently referenced definition that describes the profession as "the management function that identifies, establishes, and maintains mutually beneficial relationships between an organization and the various publics on whom its success or failure depends" (Bruning, 2001, as cited by Cutlip, Center, and Broom, 1985, p.4).

Battling for support among academia and the corporate world, public relation scholars have multiple theories that encourage the need for a strong OP relationship. For PR practitioners, the opportunity to form a relationship with the public involves a sizeable amount of support from the reputation of the organization, the level of satisfaction achieved from the consumer, and the ability for an individual to identify the product offered and the company behind it (Hong & Yang, 2009). By overseeing relationship building, marketing, and communication among company publics, it is up to the PR professional to make sure that all channels of communication are clear and accessible. When stakeholders see an organization as attractive, their perception of a positive reputation increases, presenting the potential for identification and relationship support (Hong & Yang, 2009, as cited by Bhattarcharya & Elsbach, 2002).

Addressing the public. Organizations that adhere to PR influence and CRM practices also understand the importance of communication in relationship management, and as a result, can determine which approach works best with a specific audience. Grunig and Grunig's (1989) *Towards a Theory of PR* describes the various methods of communication used by a PR practitioner to provide organizational information to members of the public. Because of the vast amount of theories available for PR practitioners to apply within the field, four major models of communication are discussed that can occur between organizations and its publics: press agentry, public information, two-way asymmetrical and two-way symmetrical. When using press agentry, the traditional associations of propaganda and media representation are the driving force behind relationship development, while the public information process (also described as the "in-house" journalist) relays a more informative and truthful depiction of organizational information, but from the perspective of the organization.

Both press agentry and public information are one-way symmetrical channels that direct communication only from the organization to the public, as opposed to two-way asymmetrical and two-way symmetrical, which enables the organization's use of research as the basis for its communicative messages, while the other uses cooperation and compromise tactics to encourage settlements, respectively (Grunig &Grunig, 1989). While two-way symmetrical approaches are typically favored, an organization's PR department must be ready to utilize any of these tactics, as the structure of a specific industry may call for a more traditional or modern approach towards processing information for their publics.

Consumer identification & word-of-mouth tactics. Public Relations has transcended beyond traditional aspects of publicity and media, into a managing component for organizations to strategically plan and develop relationships with members of the public (Grunig, 2006). In order to initiate business-to-business (B2B) or business-to-consumer (B2C) relationships, PR practitioners must recognize the importance of market structure and preferred communication. Knowledge of which communicative channels are preferred from consumers can assist in identifying the social environments of stakeholders, consumers, and its publics. When PR personnel are cognizant of the number of competitors within the industry, the varying incomes of consumers, the level of activity among publics, and the source of branding among consumers, the organization achieves the perfect opportunity to efficiently distinguish their customers. It is when all affiliated stakeholders feel as though they are important assets to the company that personal identification and social support of the organization increases their overall satisfaction (Smith, Drumwright & Gentile, 2010). Smith et al (2010) discuss how important market identification can be in their article *The New Marketing Myopia*. The use of the term 'myopia' evolves from scenarios in which a company's interest is solely on their current customer base, without any considering all stakeholders, or the social environments that PR and marketing departments operate within. Recent limitations from companies that do not research and address stakeholder needs as a part of their marketing communication tactics have shown signs of diminished loyalty, support, and identification, resulting in a relapse of market influence (Smith et al, 2010).

With a solid understanding of public relations, an organization will have a plethora of communication strategies and approaches for creating, sustaining, and managing relationships between organizations and their publics. Just as one must know which calculated channel of communication is best suited for a population segment, the tactics used to inform the messages to the individuals is just as important. Hong & Yang (2009) recognized the simplicity of interpersonal conversations held by way of word-of-mouth (WOM), and the impact conversations have among a population. WOM can heavily affect customer-company identification, and when positively received, supports an increase of satisfaction with a company. As WOM occurs, PR departments who directly disperse practitioners to communicate with stakeholders are able to progress the relationship development between company and customers, who in return, increase the identification rates with the organization (Hong & Yang, 2009).

Public relations and issue management. The communication role of public relations during a crisis is crucial to the organization's ability to save customer retention, market value, and overall reputation. Crisis situations occur when there is an unexpected scenario that has the potential to damage stakeholder and public relationships, as well as the image and status of the organization (Ihlen, 2010). The best PR tactics have proven to assist organization-public relationships in times of need. During these situations, PR practitioners must communicate with all stakeholders with clear instructions of the reasons why the issue occurred, how each stage of the crisis is being managed, and what the organization is doing to resolve the issue. If ever a point comes where a critical situation occurs, resulting in an unavoidable crisis, the best organizations with strong PR practitioners have managed their relationships, retained stakeholders, and engendered public support because they were able to anticipate impeding disasters and prepare constituents beforehand (Ihlen, 2010).

Due to influxes in stakeholder and public interest, the PR professional's ability to manage relationships must be keen to alterations and uncertainty. Van Leuven & Slater (1991) go into great detail on communication processes PR professionals use to manage media and publics relationships. The authors make the claim that an accomplished PR practitioner should acknowledge the continuously changing nature of organizations, publics, and the environment, and in the process they too must change the methods and tactics used to develop and sustain working relationships. A five-point process for opinion shaping is provided, explaining the stages used by PR practitioners that can effectively manage an organization and members of the public via media involvement: Awareness (limited group awareness), Elaboration (development and increased knowledge), Understanding (synthesized issues and alignment with sides), Attitude Crystallization (set groups, increased media attention), and Action (lobbying, negotiation, intense media coverage). The better understanding the PR practitioner has regarding public opinion, the better they will be able to address media, providing opportunities to state clear and effective organizational positions in a situation (Van Leuven & Slater, 1991).

Relationship Management

Origins of relationship management. As the
accountabilities for PR practitioners increase, the
profession has grown to presume managerial training as a
basic foundation of their experience. As this expectancy
grows, the applicability of PR communication, theories,
and CRM programs are increasingly being used to solve
company issues, presenting new opportunities for OP
relationships to expand among customers, employees and
stakeholders (Ledingham, 2003). Relationship
management (RM) is a crucial component to any form of
organizational growth with stakeholders and publics. RM
assists in establishing the path of communication between
organizational-public (OP) relationships, while analyzing
responses and determining the personal values expressed
from segments of the population (Bruning, 2001).
Unfortunately, because of the high number of mass-media
oriented practitioners, there is a still lack of managerial
procedures among the field of practitioners who recognize
the role RM has upon organization-public relationships.

Relationship Management is a theory that positions
public relations as the medium in facilitating the interests
of an organization and its publics by managing all public
relationships (Ledingham, 2003). Pioneering the aspects
of RM, Ledingham (2003) instituted a belief of PR as a
managerial function that goes beyond the traditional
assumptions associated with the field, stating " In the
relational perspective, relationship presuppositions act as
a framing mechanism for theory building, teaching, and
practice" (p. 188). The relational perspective offered
describes communication outcomes that are developed
from PR departments with members of the public in mind.
Four developmental aspects of PR frameworks assist in the
management of organizational-public relationships: 1)

24

Relationships development must be a center role of PR; 2)
PR must be recognized as a management operation to truly
be effective; 3) PR and RM practitioners must identify
stakeholder and publics components to connect attitudes
and perceptions; and 4) PR and RM models must be
organized to accommodate all members of an
organization's public (Ledingham, 2003). The relational
perspectives of RM generate positive associations between
organization and publics, which aid in measuring future
relational dimensions of trust, openness, involvement,
investment and commitment (Ledingham, 2003).

*Internal and external relationship
management.* Relational dimensions are a cornerstone
of RM development because of the personal attributes that
can support or destroy a relationship between
organizations and their publics. Due to the continued
questioning of relevance regarding PR activities,
researchers and organizations have focused on ways OP
relationships are able to determine imprints of public and
stakeholder satisfaction. Relational dimensions of trust
("comfort" ability between organization and public),
openness (how much and how often information is
exchanged), involvement (visibility of organization among
the public), investment (social/infrastructural/financial
support to the public) and commitment (consistency of
communication) are used to determine if a relationship
exists, with each dimension supporting a pillar for OP
relationship development (Bruning & Ledingham, 1998).
So long as PR practitioners take these relational
dimensions into account when forming and addressing
members of the public, there is an enormous opportunity
to secure loyalty among stakeholders and publics.

A final perspective on the source of RM influence is rooted among employee levels of satisfaction when representing an organization. Because of their position as direct representatives of an organization, the attitudes and beliefs held by those who work for a company have the ability to shape a customer's portrayal of an organization (Lindenmann, 1998). When employees are displeased with the organization, their RM capabilities can become skewed, due to a lack of support or belief in company perspectives (Lindenmann, 1998). RM can only work when those who are responsible for maintaining OP relationships are content with their positions and can generate positive feelings about the organization. In return, organizations with employees who think in favor of their organization also encourage internal communication, fulfilling the needs of satisfaction for both employees and publics (Lindenmann, 2003).

Relationship Management and Customer Relationship Management
Integration and critiques. Public Relations has the ability to ascend beyond a traditional means of publicity and media into a managing component for organizations to strategically plan and develop relationships with stakeholders and the consumer populations (Grunig, 2006). It is because of a PR practitioner's versatility that RM goes hand-in-hand with current trends of PR facilitation, but other organizational functions share similar expectations of relationship development, satisfaction and retention. Throughout PR studies, authors have proposed that PR perceptions grow when stakeholders are identified and separated for individual assessments and evaluations (Grunig, 2006). As mentioned before, CRM connections to PR and RM

help in instituting communicative channels through program applications that increase the OP relationships between consumer and provider (Nakra, 2000). Because the overarching goal of CRM is to produce consumers who will become life-long consumers, the importance of satisfying stakeholders simplifies the consumer's need for cognition, increasing the opportunity to make the consumer a repeater purchaser of goods and services (Nakra, 2000).

When used as a tool for relationship management, the benefits of CRM programs are still ambiguous, receiving both praise and criticism depending upon the implementation process. Reinartz, Krafft, and Hoyer (2004) go into great depth discussing the applicability of CRM program and its wavering effects produced over the years. While some have come to praise CRM processes for achievements within business structure, others doubt its true relevance from a lack of tangible evidence and consistently alternating set of program results. CRM has a direct correlation with relational management because of programs that identify and retrieve customer data, providing organizations with information to influence customer relationships. With early projections since the early 2000's that have estimated total spending on CRM programs to be a multi-billion dollar industry (Elliot, 2002), CRM programs are successful, but only when the implementation process is supported by a management system that will oversee the initiation, maintenance, and termination (by way of customer-organization relationships) (Reinartz et al, 2004).

Customer contact techniques. Relationship Management and CRM are founded on the shared premise of customer preservation, with each term recognizing the importance of public interactions to stimulate organizational productivity. Because of a customer's request for a certain level of accessibility to an organization, the public relation framework allows for RM and CRM to do its job by determining what aspects of a business satisfies or displeases its publics. Researchers have established theories that predict OP satisfaction levels are drawn from correlations between customer expectations and preference, quality of service vs. reduced preference, rationality vs. quality, and additional comparisons, all of which can be subjected to traditional marketing innovation of product development (Rust, Inman, Jia, & Zahorik, 1999). When companies bolster their communicative relationships through consumer evaluations and public perceptions, their ability to contact customers via direct marketing (mailings, promotions, tangible incentives) or through online media (emails, websites, social media) alters the individual attention each stakeholder segment receives. General CRM allots for the personalization of programming per user (such as sign in sheets at events, open ended questionnaires, incentives for participation), while online CRM programs are effective (click-through advertisements, promotional incentives, emails, blogs and e-subscriptions), as long as customers feel their information remains private (Horn, Feinberg & Salvendy, 2005).

Conversations in Communication ®
Volume II

Customer Relationship Management (CRM) as a Function of Public Relations

LIST OF THE MOST POPULAR CRM TOOLS:

Direct mailings, emails, advertisements, surveys, automated service channels, transaction kiosks, opinion polls, incentive based activities, reward and loyalty systems, preferred customer packages, warranty programs, press conferences, cloud storage.

TYPICAL ACCESS POINTS FOR CRM WITH AN ORGANIZATION:

operator-based services, self-service, online communication (see types of CRM assistance).

CRM PROGRAMS ARE MANAGED IN THREE WAYS:

IN HOUSE DEPARTMENTS

OUTSOURCED TO COMPANIES

PURCHASED SOFTWARE

THREE MAJOR FUNCTIONS OF CRM:

MARKETING

SALES

CUSTOMER SERVICE

CRM tactics and outlets include, but are not limited to, direct mailings, emails, advertisements, surveys, automated service channels (ex. Internet access, phone and voice recognition programs), transaction kiosks (Sun, 2006, p. 594),

opinion polls, incentive based activities, reward and loyalty systems, preferred customer packages, warranty programs, and press conferences (Venkatesan, Kumar, & Bohling, 2007; Fletcher, 2003; Boulding et al, 2005).

Many of the programs listed above are often used in conjunction with another, and practiced by virtually every department within an organization (West, 2001; Khalifa & Shenn, 2009; Tanner et al, 2005; Fletcher, 2003).

CRM functions may be operator-based services (such as call center and mailings), self-service (leaflets, ATMs) (Sun, 2006),

based entirely online via eCRM (web pages, access to forms, information) (Horn, Feinberg, & Salvendy, 2005),

or include all of the above, depending upon the budget and access allotted from an organization for CRM development. The CRM programs themselves are either created through in-house departments (IT, marketing), outsourced through hired consultants, or purchase program packets for implementation (Sun, 2006)."

-Jabaree Dunham-Carson

Relationship Management and Corporate Social Responsibility

Relationship management assists in facilitating CRM's capability to function as a theoretical construct of public relations, and helps to mold the profession into a consumer-response seeking, managerial task that harks upon the needs of its stakeholders. For this connection between businesses and publics to sustain itself, the organization is likely (to a certain extent) to provide its publics with a sense of community investment, as means to show support to segments who have directly, or indirectly, supported the organization's growth. Along with RM, Corporate Social Responsibility (CSR) is the level of influence, innovations, or services from an organization that contributes to members of society, which in return, has the ability to improve customer perceptions and financial commitments (Luo & Bhattacharya, 2006). Examples of CSR occur when a company erects a building to provide non-profit services an area to operate within; purchasing large quantities of food and medical supplies to assist a population in need; creating a new product or service that reduces the amount of paper needed for its production, saving thousands of trees, and many other public services that fall under the form of corporate philanthropy. Kotler and Lee (2004) discuss how several organizations that recognize how important CSR values are from a consumer perspective. Over 90% of *Fortune* 500 companies institute CSR initiatives (Lichtenstein, Drumwright, and Bridgette 2004), several of which have donations that exceed $100 million dollars (Berner 2005, p.72). Forming a cyclical process, when an organization has low levels of innovation, the CSR prospects goes down, affecting the organization's market share; when innovation is high, increased CSR values are assumed.

The majority of studies that follow the impact of CSR upon organizational implementation generate attention toward the quality and uniqueness of a product or service, the potential cost upon the consumer , the service itself, or the overall accessibility of a product to the public (Bruning & Ledingham, 1998).When an organization gives back, whether it is providing a product that redefines an industry, or providing additional assistance in resolving a sociological issue, the role of corporate philanthropy and corporate community relations is well received if the organization appears genuine among the public and consumers. PR practitioners and their dominant coalition must insure that trust and credibility appear from the organization to each segment of stakeholders, along with distinguishable channels of two-way communication. This awareness indicates clear depictions of community commitment from the organization to ensure the development of strong B-2-C relationships (Hall, 2006). When comparing stakeholders who are directly affiliated with the company (customers) to those who are aware of how much the company gives back (members of the general public), the chance of strengthening customer awareness and OP relationships increase via CSR activities and recognition.

Relational perspective of customer relationship management. When considering the vast amount of OP relationships that are monitored by a public relations department, Ledingham's (2003) relational perspective of RM can be used as the blueprint for strategizing effective and socially involved communication, while simultaneously segmenting members of the general population. It is because of the interchangeability of PR theory that the concepts of CRM and CSR can theoretically be fastened to RM's relational perspective. When considering the four components of the relational perspective, two of the axioms (recognition of relationship development as a PR function; identification of stakeholders/publics for attitudinal perceptions) run parallel with principles of CRM protocol and implementation. Both RM and CRM share a consumer-driven goal of amplifying customer retention rates as a way to expand financial profit and organizational growth (Lindenmann, 1998). Public relations departments can easily capitalize upon increasing CRM capabilities by way of RM, as the responses from CRM programming provide the attitudinal responses needed to gather consumer information (Nakra, 2000). This allows a company to categorize and establish public and stakeholder segments, and market the satisfaction levels of individuals to targeted populations.   Unified through the assistance of RM's process of identifying publics, stakeholders in return simplify purchasing habits, increasing retention rates and customer longevity based on CRM provided] information, and gather attitudes and reputation testimonies from past consumers.

The remaining two developmental aspects of RM's relational perspective theory (relation management by PR professionals; PR/RM models must be crafted for all OP relationships) easily corresponds with the public-serving notions of CSR. Public relations has grown beyond a term and position limited to marketing departments, but has become enthralled into everyday managerial, technical, and even political positions. When organizations attempt to introduce CSR driven community involvement, management must be prepared to handle all segments of the public with a clear understanding of the issues at hand, explanations of what needs to be addressed, and have a resolution in works. Unfortunately, many organizations grossly underestimate the amount of influence that PR professionals can have serving as a public representative throughout local communities (Wise, 2007). When considering CSR as a utility of RM, a business can institute PR techniques by facilitating communication of company contributions through media outlets and direct correspondence between the organization and the community. This action would allow the PR practitioner to shape the communicative models for assessing publics. As a company achieves stability between adhering to community members while meeting their own financial obligations, support for CSR is justified, and relational management can continue to benefit stakeholder and public satisfaction.

The role of PR in management goes beyond simply serving as a conduit between the organization and the public, but as the entity to ensure both sides receives the support necessary to achieve satisfaction. CRM programs and CSR initiatives assist in enhancing an organization's public support and consumer information. Unfortunately, without proper relational management from PR practitioners and the dominant coalition, the two are severely limited. Public relations models and programs imposed upon stakeholders and publics must provide the best line of support possible to sustain positive OP relationships, which is a necessary objective if any future advances in customer service, consumer satisfaction, or retention are to occur.

Chapter III

Influence in Direct Communication Processes Technologies and Programs

Sun (2006) addresses the design and focus of many CRM programs in the article *Technology Innovation and Implications for Customer Relationship Management*, identifying the communicative goals used for measuring CS, retention rates, customer life cycle (CLC) and WOM support (Boulding, Staelin, Ehret, & Johnston, 2005). These various techniques are used by management to sustain a strong public identification and secure stakeholder relationships. The expansive nature of CRM has allowed organizations to improve upon communication tactics by reconstructing the customer-relationship process and inspiring new approaches from salespersons to consumers. In order to discover what is necessary for an OP relationship to flourish via CRM, these new methods of communication must include forms of media used by organizations to connect with publics, as well accessible outlets to be used by customers for individual involvement. Several CRM scholars suggest that organizations who emphasize CRM development often direct their communication toward market and sales automation, call centers, E- Commerce and web design, field services, and customer-firm affection (Sun, 2006;Yim, Tse, & Chan, 2008). As the information is collected, communication analyst will evaluate the success and failure of program implementation effectiveness (Tanner, Donthu, Gardner, Krishnamurthy, & Noble, 2005; Khalifa & Shen, 2009).

CRM tactics and outlets include, but are not limited to, direct mailings, emails, advertisements, surveys, automated service channels (ex. Internet access, phone and voice recognition programs), transaction kiosks (Sun, 2006, p. 594), opinion polls, incentive based activities, reward and loyalty systems, preferred customer packages, warranty programs, and press conferences (Venkatesan, Kumar, & Bohling, 2007; Fletcher, 2003; Boulding et al, 2005). Many of the programs listed above are often used in conjunction with another, and practiced by virtually every department within an organization (West, 2001; Khalifa & Shenn, 2009; Tanner et al, 2005; Fletcher, 2003). CRM functions may be operator-based services (such as call center and mailings), self-service (leaflets, ATMs) (Sun, 2006), based entirely online via eCRM (web pages, access to forms, information) (Horn, Feinberg, & Salvendy, 2005), or include all of the above, depending upon the budget and access allotted from an organization for CRM development. The CRM programs themselves are either created through in-house departments (IT, marketing), outsourced through hired consultants, or purchase program packets for implementation (Sun, 2006).

Customer and Company Investments

Every industry is akin to some form of CRM protocol, as more firms and organizations begin to focus attention to retain customer satisfaction. Sun (2006) continues elaborating the methodologies behind the more 'well known' CRM activities, explaining the apparent goals of CRM promotion and incentives. As customers receive information regarding a product or service, the decision of whether or not to continue services with an organization can be influenced by potential rewards offered through service upgrades, additional products, and assured assistance. The CRM influence of incentives and endorsement encourages the future of a customer's identification with an organization, while priming the

consumer to anticipate future promotions from the
organization, keeping the CLC in motion (West, 2001).

Over the years CRM programs, tactics, and
techniques have grown from a simple concept of customer-
driven communication, to a lucrative marketing
philosophy, ameliorating our initial perspectives of how an
organization connects with its stakeholders. Elliot's
(2001) research measures company investments in CRM
funding from the early mid-to-late 1990's to mid 2000's,
and found that CRM industry sales increased from
$2.8billion in 1998, to projections of over $16.8 billion in
2003 (p. 49). In 2005, there were five major CRM
programs mentioned in the *Statistically Speaking* (2006)
column pertaining to CRM growth and product market
share. The top five organizations generated nearly
$3.5billion alone, with SAP (Systems Analysis and
Program Development) generating over $1.4 billion, Siebel
systems with $966 million, and Oracle with $367 million.
The CRM programs offered from Salesforce.com and
Amdocs rounded out the top five with $280 million, and
with $276 million, respectively (Statistically Speaking,
2006, p. 16).

Organizations that produce CRM programs have the
potential to generate significant levels of profit. Companies
that purchase CRM tools may spend as much as $3,000
per user simply upon registration, while other products
such as BroadVision will cost an organization $400,000 to
purchase (Elliot, 2001, p.44). There are several
inexpensive or free products via open source programs for
organizations that cannot afford to spend such large
amounts of funding on their CRM strategies. Open source
products allow users to download publicly available
programs, but because of the limited services available for
assistance, they are often criticized. Brandon (2009)

describes some of the most reputable and inexpensive open source CRM programs such as SugarCRM, a free CRM program that has several users who voluntarily assist other users via forum discussions, and Zoho CRM Pro, which provides additional marketing features, and only charges $12 per user each month (p. 48).

Research suggests that organizations recognize the value of customer identification in order to capitalize profit potential, while the customers capitalize upon the services offered (Boulding et al, 2005). Boulding et al, (2005) go on to suggest that a company that invests in CRM must go beyond merely selling the product but must also create the value of customer satisfaction, and through CS, the organization is able to survive and produce for future customers (p. 156). As with PR practitioners, Boulding et al, (2005) make claim that CRM strategies must formulate and analyze how customers, competitors, and the company itself, provide information to make the overall experience for the consumer progressive and pleasing.

Conversations in Communication ®
Volume II

Customer Relationship Management (CRM) as a Function of Public Relations

CRM AND SOCIAL MEDIA:

2008

72% of social media users will engage in some form of CRM within their social networks.

72%

55% of CRM Market share was controlled by four companies (leading companies include Salesforce.com, Microsoft, and Oracle).

salesforce   Microsoft   ORACLE

When companies use their CRM capabilities to connect with social media networks, there is a large return on the investment, with 72% of their participants intending to connect to their social networks through their CRM programs within a year **(Arman, 2014, as cited by Blackenhorn, 2011). In 2008,**

the majority of the CRM market was led by four companies who collectively held **55 percent** share of control **(Wang et al, 2013, as cited by Gartner, 2009).**

55%

Of these companies, SalesForce.com and Microsoft are known for their total inclusion of cloud, social media, and mobile based CRM applications."
-Jabaree Dunham-Carson

Measurement Process

As research to connect CRM and relationship development increases, authors continue to establish the empirical connections between the public reputation of an organization and the ways satisfaction influences consumer relationships. Brønn (2008) believes that a struggle ensues among PR professionals who wish to revitalize the communicative process of satisfying individuals first, rather than the traditional focus of using the reputation of the organization to please consumers. Brønn's (2008) evaluation of the organization MartinFidem, determined that the indications of measuring a successful relationship depends upon the organization's ability to recognize the impact that trust, control mutuality, commitment, and satisfaction have toward relationship reinforcement. Trust measurements are used to determine the amount of assurance between organizations and publics, based upon facets of integrity (fairness), dependability (consistency) and competence (proof of dedication). Control mutuality can be measured to test how malleable the direction of the relationship can be, depending on the situation (Is the organization in control the communication, or will their public(s) command the flow of communication?) (Brønn, 2008).

Brønn (2008) continues to explore this communicative process by way of CRM and RM, recognizing the financial and emotional exchange between PR professionals, organizations, and publics that emphasize relational commitment and satisfaction. When commitment is high, both the organization and its publics will consistently reinvest within one another due to continuance commitment (repetitive action of progression) and affective commitments (emotional involvement). When all aspects of the relationship are assessed, satisfaction measurements will explore the levels of content from both customer and provider (Brønn, 2008). The positive results incurred from the study promoted future research for relationship measurements via customer relationships, supporting the position of CRM measurements as an ideal tool for PR facilitation.

Customer Consideration

Organizations that adapt and implement CRM programs are pioneers in the fields of marketing and PR research because they believe in the foundation of support surrounding the development of OP relationships. Recognizing the importance of B2B and B2C transactions, West (2001) critiques the CRM process from a customers' perspective, and gives consideration to role initial contact (via product or marketing) has on consumer purchasing, and CRM programs that communicate with customers post-purchase (Sun, 2006). Sun's (2006) study on CRM technology and innovations suggest that CRM programs reach beyond primary relationship development, providing organizations and marketers a gauge that can determine the impressions of their sales approach. These CRM features can be used to evaluate consumer purchasing strategies, or assist in predicting which products are likely to be purchased based on customer information provided.

Customers who have had positive experiences with an organization are often repeat clients who are likely to succumb to the recurring pattern of the customer life cycle (CLC). Combining the principle components of CRM (marketing, service, and sales), the goal of the cycle is to position marketing tactics for securing sales, after which new prominence toward providing excellent customer service becomes the new focus, only to once again determine marketing strategies to promote new items, etc.,

(Sun, 2006). From a PR perspective, securing customer placement upon the CLC allows the organization to better equip their CRM applications and reinforce the communication process between the customer and provider.

Successes and Failures

As with any strategic plan, the success of CRM programming is incumbent upon the effort put into sustaining, monitoring, and evaluating the process of implementation. CRM is no different from any operational plan, and will produce results that mirror the amount of support given from higher management and the dominant coalition. The study from Homburg, Hoyer, and Stock (2007) focuses on revival tactics via CRM programming, arguing that the programs and strategies that have worked for many organizations will depend upon the designs of the program, as well as knowledge of their customer base in order to keep the CLV high and the CLC in motion. In contrast, Lemon et al, (2002) study on CRM and future-focused considerations claim that customers must look beyond their present association, and anticipate future usage of a product or service in order to support CRM usage. When Woodside & Delozier (1976) discuss perceived risk among consumers, successful CRM will always position program intentions toward providing consumers with ways to eliminate concerns, and produce customers who feel their CRM information is secure and their input is beneficial (Bauer, 1960).

There are members of academia who question the purpose of CRM programming due to a range of vague definitions and consistently redefined expectations. Reimann et al (2010) highlight the failure rates of CRM projects to be as high as 70%, either producing losses for a company or no substantial improvement (The Gartner Group, 2003). Continuing their evaluation of CRM and its impact on organizational performance, Reimann et al (2010) assessed several industries and analyzed their CRM programs, conducting several interviews and surveys, only to conclude that CRM may not necessarily be the 'boost' needed to improve the CS quality of an organization. The results of CRM are often two ways, resulting in a reduction of CLV, due to irrelevant connections and inconsistencies of CRM programs (Reimann et al, 2010).

When an organization provides the best quality of care, ease of access, and open communication, stakeholders and publics will benefit from customer-firm affections (Yim et al, 2008). 'Customer-firm affections' is a term used to describe the relationship an individual has when they choose to affiliate with an organization on a personal level (Yim et al, 2008). CRM is fully capable of producing such an effect; however, this particular execution within an organization entails a complete revival of organizational structure and attitudes towards the perception of the customer (Boulding et al, 2005).

Over the years, CRM has consistently been subjected to reviews and critiques in order to make programs more efficient and supportive. In recent times, the organizations that have successfully incorporated CRM are noted for their increase in overall organizational performance, due to CRM's ability to assist the needs of consumers due to communication tools that extend beyond traditional marketing (Krasnikov, Jaychandran, & Kumar, 2009). As mentioned before, CRM implementation can be costly, depending on which programs are used, but as more packages become available, the CRM market offers a variety of programs that can meet a wide range of organizational budgets (Elliot, 2001).

Scholars and researchers are becoming more confident in findings that support correlations between CRM programs, the creation of customer satisfaction, and the increase in organizational profit. Krasnikov et al (2009) suggest that firms who are doubtful of CRM must remember the influence that a strong OP relationship can have in creating customer identification. The CRM implementation process can boost the profit efficiency of an organization, despite the cost to incorporate the program (Krasnikov et al, 2009). CRM has the ability to assist in the identification of company publics, recognize CLV processes, and augment customer communication, and its implementation must be supported by PR practitioners, managers, and members of the dominant coalition.

Ryals (2005) praises CRM as a necessary component to PR, Marketing, and CS, (Day, 2004), but also recognizes the potential for failure in producing results when there is little managerial support (as cited by Zablah, Bellenger, and Johnston, 2004). The role of management and CRM implementation must be seen as a channel to focus the attention of employees not only upon the product offered from an organization, but to the experience and services offered with association. Previous research from Lemon, White, and Winer (2002) proposed that a customer's decision to continue a relationship with an organization will depend on past, present, and future evaluations of organizational performance, by way of customer satisfaction, service quality, and the perception of quality (p.1). It is because of the need to sustain the customer life cycle that all forms of management are responsible for promoting CRM tools and programs as "a solution that enhances the effectiveness of firm's customer relationship strategies than as a means to achieve quick cost reduction..." (Krasnikov et al, 2009 p.72).

Research Questions and Hypotheses

As public relations continues to professionally and academically escalate, the managerial prospective of the practitioner must also evolve. Continued support among RM and CRM theories must encourage combining elements throughout the entire realm of communication to uplift the exchange between an organization and the public. For future studies of PR and RM, researchers should seek to discover how mediated communication to publics and stakeholders is managed from an organizational perspective.

Are there specially trained public representatives who serve as spokespersons or moderators when addressing CSR issues, or is someone simply sent from the organization? Researchers may also want to explore the impact of CRM as a public relations tool regarding accessibility via marketing tactics (emails, surveys, testimonies). Do the respondents feel as though the organization is genuinely considerate of their needs, or do they believe their involvement in CRM programming is oriented asymmetrically, with communication delivered only from organization to consumer? Are customers simply pumped for information via CRM programming, with the results from the data collected only to be used for organizational gain?

RQ1: Which channels of communication support the best CRM relationships?
RQ2: Are respondents aware of what an organization's CSR activities are?

When considering the ways attitudes, loyalty, satisfaction, and retention can influence intentions and association, there is very little research that corresponds with the PR profession and CRM development. There are presumptions from theories that suggest attitudes, subjective norms and perceived control will encourage the intention to perform the expected behavior, by way of the Theory of Planned Behavior (Ajzen, 2002). Yet even if intentions are strong, the assumptions of TPB relationships may not support actual behavioral change or control in a situation (Bansal & Taylor, 2002). Oliver and Bearden (1985) reference Miniard and Cohen (1979, 1981, 1983) who argue that there is little evidence to support to connections of attitudes and behavior via TPB, while Ajzen and Driver (1992) professed that attitudes in select situations may have influence on intention at one point, but have little to no effect, in another.

> **RQ3: What are the services that encourage a customer to associate with a particular organization?**
> **RQ4: Are organizations given higher ratings of approval if they have maintained contact with their customers?**

Bansal and Taylor's (2002) research on customers who switch their service providers concluded that affiliation with their service provider has a strong correlation to how an individual identifies with a product. With knowledge of PR functionality and CRM programs, how can organizations take relational cues from CRM, RM and PR strategies and implement them to stakeholders to improve their OP relationships and manage their communication tactics?

The following hypotheses were proposed:

H1: Respondents who see their banks as credible will have a higher level of overall satisfaction with their bank.

H2: Respondents who perceive their banking provider has a good reputation will have a higher level of satisfaction.

H3: Respondents who identify more strongly with their banking providers will have a positive perception of the bank's customer communication practices.

Chapter IV

Method:

The goal of this research was to discover if a link existed between Customer Relationship Management (CRM) programs and their ability to serve as a function of Public Relations when developing stakeholder relationships. The inquiry to successfully answer the proposed research questions and hypotheses depended on the researcher's ability to compare and analyze organizational perceptions from active customers. The decision to study banking communication resulted from careful consideration of which industries were virtually accessible to every member of society. Individuals from the research population were expected to have some form of affiliation with a banking provider, or received some form of direct communication during their relationship with the organization. Once the surveys were completed, the responses were evaluated.

Participants

There were 100 individuals who participated in the study. Participants were selected via nonrandom convenience sampling using the snowball sampling technique. The sample population selected included individuals who are affiliated with the University of Hartford (students, employees, affiliates), as well as the personal networks among those who chose to participate.

Recruitment

Participants were asked to complete an online survey that was accessible through active links among social media platforms and email messages. Using 'status updates' on social networks such as Facebook, Google +,

Twitter, and Tumblr, the survey links were available and viewed as 'posts' that connected participants from their social media accounts or emails to the survey homepage. 'Status updates' were also reposted and shared by additional members of the participant's social network as a way to increase the number of partakers, supporting the 'snowball' technique. An example of a potential status update/post used to encourage participation in the survey included: "Are you happy with your banking provider? Tell us your thoughts."

Each link had a brief description of the survey and allowed the reader the opportunity to participate in the survey. All participants were then redirected to the survey hosted by the website "surveymonkey.com", and consent forms were provided to all participants (see Appendix B). If participants wanted a copy of the consent form, one would be forwarded to them by notifying the researcher via email. All participants confirmed that they have understood the purpose of the research, and were above the age of 18.

Participants then completed the survey which was broken into four sections: (1) Demographic information, (2) organizational reputation, (3) organizational assimilation, and (4) source credibility (See Appendix C). Questions that were irrelevant to the purpose of the study were excluded or slightly modified to achieve the best assessment of the banking industry.

Instruments

Participants began the first section by answering basic demographic information (ex: sex, ethnicity, income), followed by their current educational status, and current banking experience. Samples of banking experience questions include "Do you currently have a

checking/savings account?" and "How would you rate your
current banking experience in terms of?" The next series
of questions provided the researcher with the level of
communication between the bank and the customer, and
how often the banking provider contacts the customer.
Examples of this include "How often do you contact your
banking provider each year?" and "What is your preferred
form of communication with your banking provider?"
Participants were then asked questions regarding their
bank's CSR activity ("Were you aware of the attempted
monthly debit card usage fee that would be charged to
customers?"), in addition to ranking their preference of
communication from their bank, and which banking
features they use ("What banking services do you
utilize?").

Section two in the survey measured the level of
influence that attitudes have upon social perceptions and
CSR, and RM communication. Coombs & Holladay's
(1996) Organization Reputation Scale is 10-item
instrument, modified from McCroskey's (1966) character
scale of ethos measurement. The scale explores how the
public image of an organization can be perceived as the
organization's 'character' among its customers.
Modifications were made to the scale to reflect the
communication between banking organizations and their
customers. Sample items from the scale included: "I do
trust the organization to tell the truth about any incidents",
and "The organization is concerned with the well-being of
its publics?" The scale was constructed using a five-point
likert scale, with responses ranging from 1(strongly
disagree) to 5 (strongly agree). The reliability coefficients
from past studies ranged from .81 to .92.

The third section of the survey focused upon
discerning the motivation behind customer association

and identification with their banking provider. Participants answered questions from the 20 item Organizational Assimilation Index (OAI) (Myers & Oetzel, 2003). The scale was created to determine which factors assist in measuring association, providing six dimensions for surveying: familiarity with supervisors, organizational acculturation, recognition, involvement, job competency, and role negotiation. Modifications were made to the scale in order to reflect the communication between banking organizations and their customers. For the purpose of the study, items regarding the dimensions of "familiarity with supervisors" was changed to "familiarity with banking provider" (ex. "I feel like I know my supervisor pretty well" became "I feel like I know my banking provider pretty well"), while "job competency" items was excluded from the survey. A total of 15 items from the original 20 were included, excluding the four from the "job competency" section, and one from the role negotiation section. The scale was constructed using a five-point likert scale, with responses ranging from 1(strongly disagree) to 5 (strongly agree). The reliability coefficients from past studies ranged from .62 to .86 among the six dimensions.

The final section of the questionnaire completed the survey by analyzing perceptions of PR/OP involvement using the 18 item Measure of Source Credibility (Teven & McCroskey, 1997; McCroskey & Teven, 1999). The authors believe that the scale would assist in research to measure how competence, goodwill, and trustworthiness are primary components used to establish likeability and support for an organization. Modifications were made to the scale in order to reflect the communication between banking organizations and their customers. The scale was constructed using a seven-point semantic differential scale, with responses ranging from generally negative associations as 1, to generally positive associations as a 7 (with the exception of select items for reverse coding). Sample terms from the scale include: "Untrained— Trained" for competence factors, "Insensitive---Sensitive" for goodwill factors, and "Phony---Genuine" for trustworthiness factors. 9 of the 18 items were reverse coded. The reliability coefficients from past studies ranged from .85 to .92, with a .94 alpha for the overall scale.

Results:
Data Analysis (Research Questions)

After the responses were collected, the survey data was analyzed in order to determine whether or not there was any evidence that supports a connection between CRM programs, Public Relation tactics, and OP relationships. Because of participant drop out at different points, there are various sample sizes recorded throughout the analysis. Frequency analyses were used to evaluate responses for RQ's 1-3. Pearson Correlations were generated for RQ 4.

RQ1: Which channels of communication support the best CRM relationships?

This question explored which communication channels provided the best relationship for CRM activity. A frequency analysis (N=78) from participants reported that the most preferred CRM communication channel was to speak directly with customer representatives (services from actual people within the bank) (n=40). The second most preferred CRM communication channel was online banking services (n=25), and the third most preferred CRM communication channel was mobile banking (cell phone applications, phone calls) (n=10). The fourth preferred communication outlet were emails (n=7) and the least preferred CRM communication is the use of direct mailings (n=6) (See Table 1).

Table 1
What is your preferred form of communication with your banking provider?

Form of Communication	Preference of CRM	Frequency (n)
Direct Communication (n=79)	First	41
Online Services (n=79)	Second	25
Mobile/Tablet Applications (n=78)	Third	10
Emails (n=80)	Fourth	7
Direct Mail (Flyers, Brochures)(n=78)	Fifth	6

n=82

RQ2: Are respondents aware of what an organization's CSR activities are?

RQ2 sought to learn whether or not individuals are aware of an organization's CSR presence throughout their community, or among their social networks. The results gathered suggest that overall recognition and participation in CSR sponsored activities were relatively low, with surveys ranking as the highest form of participant involvement (n=22), followed by participation within social media (n=5). Organizational newsletters came in third (n=4) while participation in community events was the lowest recognized CSR activity (n=1) (See Table 2).

Table 2
Do you participate in any of the following activities sponsored by your
banking providers?

CSR Activity	Response %	Frequency (n)
Surveys/Questionnaires	81.5%	22
Social Media Networks (Facebook, Twitter, YouTube, etc.)	18.5%	5
Community Events (festivals, marathons benefit events, etc.)	3.7%	1
Organizational Newsletters	14.8%	4

n=27

RQ3: What are the reasons or incentives that encourage a customer to associate with a particular organization?

For RQ3, questions were asked in order to determine which services were used by participants from their banking provider. Multiple answers were accepted in order to generate a collection of banking activities per individual. The results from a frequency analysis show that the majority of participants have checking accounts (n=82), savings accounts (n=76), and debit/credit cards (n=73). There was also a good portion of participants who used their banking provider to facilitate loans (n=33) (See Table 3).

Table 3
Which banking services do your utilize?

Banking Service	Response Percent	Frequency (n)
Checking Account	98.8%	83
Savings Account	90.5%	76
Credit Union Services	23.8%	20
Money Market Account	10.7%	9
Money orders	16.7%	14
Traveler's Checks	8.3%	7
Credit/Debit Cards	88.1%	74
Foreign Currency	11.9%	10
Banking Investments (bonds/stock)	20.2%	17
Loans (auto, home, business, etc.)	39.3%	33

n=84

RQ4: Are organizations given higher ratings of approval if they have maintained contact their customers?

RQ4 explored the possible connections between organizational contact and whether or not consistent communication would influence approval of decisions. Multiple Pearson Correlations were run to compare the amount of notification the participant received from their bank, the participant's knowledge of the monthly debit charge fee, whether or not the participant agreed with the service charge, how often the individual contacts their banking provider, and the gender and ethnicity of participants. There were positive correlations between the following: gender and participant's recognition of bank notifications $r(83)$ =.224, $p<.05$; a participant's recognition of bank notifications and their awareness of the proposed monthly debit fee charge $r(82)$ =.256, $p<.05$; and customer awareness of debit fee and whether they agreed that an adequate amount of information was provided on the matter $r(80)$ =.612, $p<.001$. There was a negative correlation between gender and the participant's support for the fee increase $r(82)$ =.-251, $p<.05$. A correlation matrix summarizes results produced in Table 4. The overall correlation between bank notification and customer awareness was positive; however the majority of customers were not in support of the debit charge from their banking providers.

Customer Relationship Management (CRM) as a Function of Public Relations

Table 4

Correlations of Contact and Customer Awareness

	Variable	1	2	3	4	5	6	7	8
1	Contact (Bank)	---	.135	.115	.067	-.024	.036	-.106	.166
2	Contact (Individual)		---	.055	.081	-.109	-.059	.037	-.040
3	Sex			---	-.059	.224*	-.112	-.112	.251*
4	Ethnicity.				---	-.036	-.009	-.191	-.119
5	Notification of fees					---	.256*	.297**	-.053
6	Awareness of charge						---	.500**	.145
7	"Big 5" Notification							---	.113
8	Support of fees								---

* p < .05; **p < .001

Data Analysis (Hypotheses)

In order to examine the hypotheses one through three, Pearson correlations were used to analyze the relationships between reputation, credibility, and organizational association. As with the research question results, there were there are various sample sizes recorded throughout the analysis.

H1: Respondents who see their banks as credible will have a higher level of overall satisfaction with their bank.
The first hypothesis suggested that respondents would have a higher level of overall satisfaction with their banking provider when the organization engages in activities of goodwill. Multiple Pearson Correlations were run to compare a participant's current banking experience to their perception of that organization's source credibility, represented by the dimensions of competency credibility, goodwill credibility, and trust credibility (Teven & McCroskey, 1997). Positive correlations were assessed between the following: overall satisfaction and the dimension of goodwill credibility $r(70)$ =.258, $p<.05$. A correlation matrix summarizes results produced in Table 5.

Table 5
Current Banking Experience & Source Credibility***

	Variable	1	2	3	4	5	6
1	Overall Satisfaction	---	.268[*]	.277[*]	.036	.258[*]	.193
2	Convenience.		---	.487[**]	.124	-.261[*]	.001
3	Accessibility			---	.129	-.266[*]	.003
4	Competence Credibility				---	.193	.338[**]
5	Goodwill Credibility.					---	.415[**]
6	Trust Credibility						---

* p < .05; **p < .001

*** Source credibility is comprised from the dimensions of: competence credibility,   goodwill credibility, and trust credibility.

Results from H1 lead to an interest in exploring if there were significant relationships between a customer's banking experience, represented by convenience and accessibility, an organization's credibility, and overall satisfaction. The following positive correlations were achieved: overall satisfaction and bank accessibility $r(79)$ =.277, p<.05; overall satisfaction and banking convenience

$r(80)$ =.256, $p<.05$. Negative correlations were achieved between the following: banking convenience and goodwill credibility $r(68)$ =-.261, $p<.05$; and bank accessibility and goodwill credibility $r(67)$ =.266, $p<.05$. A correlation matrix summarizes results produced in Table 5. Overall satisfaction had a positive correlation with an organization's presence of goodwill credibility, while also correlating with customer accessibility. Banking accessibility and banking convenience had a significantly strong relationship between, but both subscales negatively correlated with goodwill credibility.

H2: Respondents who perceive their banking provider has a good reputation will have a higher level of satisfaction.

Hypothesis #2 proposed that respondents who believed their banking provider had a good reputation would report higher levels of overall satisfaction. A Pearson Correlation displayed a significant positive correlation between reputation and overall satisfaction $r(78)$ =.589, $p<.001$. There was a considerably strong correlation between the overall satisfaction associated with being a customer, and the reputation associated with their bank.

H3: Respondents who identify more strongly with their banking providers will have a positive perception of the bank's customer communication practices.

The third hypothesis anticipated that respondents who have a strong association with their banking provider would have a positive perception of their banking provider's communication. Multiple Pearson Correlations were run to compare the various levels of customer-organization assimilation, represented by the 15 item Organizational Assimilation Index (OAI) (α =.861) and the sub-dimensions of familiarity(α=.753), acculturation (culture) (α=.842), recognition(a=.895), involvement (α =.930) and role negation (α =.885) (Myers & Oetzel, 2003), with the reputation of a banking provider, the amount of times a customer has contacted their bank, and the amount of times participants received communication from their banking provider. There was no significant correlation between the reputations of an organization, and the amount of communication that occurs between banks and individuals, as reasons for perceiving positive perceptions of communication practices. Negative correlations for contact and assimilation occurred for the following: an individual's bank contact and role negotiation $r(70)$ =.277, p<.05, and the rate of bank-provided contact and acculturation $r(58)$ =-.263, $p<.05$.

The lack of support for reputation and contact led to the exploration of reputation as means for assimilation. Significantly strong correlations occurred for the following: reputation and familiarity $r(70)$ =.509, $p<.001$; reputation and recognition $r(70)$ =.680, $p<.001$; reputation and involvement $r(68)$ =.671, $p<.001$; and reputation and acculturation $r(69)$ =.639, $p<.001$.

It should be noted that the additional dimensions of the OAI scale yielded significant results when correlated among its subscales, which was anticipated. Positive correlations were reached by the following: familiarity and acculturation $r(68)$ =.728, $p<.001$; familiarity and recognition $r(69)$ =.782, $p<.001$; familiarity and involvement $r(68)$ =.785, $p<.001$; familiarity and role negotiation $r(70)$ =.293, $p<.05$; acculturation and recognition $r(68)$ =.818, $p<.001$; acculturation and involvement $r(66)$ =.764, $p<.001$; and recognition and involvement $r(68)$ =.839, $p<.001$. A correlation matrix summarizes results produced in Table 6. Overall, there were several significantly positive correlations between an individual's association with their banking provider and the perceived reputation of the organization.

Table 6
Current Banking Experience & Source Credibility***

	Variable	1	2	3	4	5	6
1	Overall Satisfaction	---	.268*	.277*	.036	.258*	.193
2	Convenience.		---	.487**	.124	-.261*	.001
3	Accessibility			---	.129	-.266*	.003
4	Competence Credibility				---	.193	.338**
5	Goodwill Credibility.					---	.415**
6	Trust Credibility						---

* p < .05; **p < .001

*** Source credibility is comprised from the dimensions of: competence credibility,   goodwill credibility, and trust credibility.

61

Discussion
Summary of Research

The purpose of this study was to research and determine whether or not Customer Relationship Management (CRM) tactics could facilitate positive Public Relations (PR) relationships between an organization and its stakeholders. Because of the discrepancies that surround CRM programming and effectiveness, surveys and scales were used to provide a customer perspective of an organization's ability to create and sustain a positive reputation, maintain communication, and provide a an overall rewarding experience. The responses were also analyzed to see if organizations could improve customer loyalty, identification, retention, and overall satisfaction by establishing strong organization-public (OP) relationships with their stakeholders. The results from this study provided new insight on the connections between CRM, PR, and OP relationships, and the information attained has the potential to benefit PR practitioners, their employers, and most importantly, the customer.

Research Questions

The first research question was asked to determine which forms of communication participants preferred from their banking provider. The most frequently reported CRM activity was direct communication, supporting earlier evidence that face-to-face communication is encouraged when establishing OP relationships. These results uphold the concept reported by Hong and Yang (2009) who proposed that organizations that incorporate Word-of-Mouth tactics via direct customer representatives have increased rates of customer identification. Participant responses consistently placed one-way asymmetrical forms of communication (such as emails and direct mailings) as their least preferred forms of contact, indicating the importance of speaking with a person, rather than simply reading literature. This low approval of asymmetrical communication is not surprising, and should signify a change from the old marketing ways of simply providing consumers with material and expecting customers to initiate communication with the organization.

The total number of responses for research question two was much smaller than anticipated, indicating low awareness of organizational CSR activities among participants. There were only 22 responses to this question; the most desired CSR activity that participants acknowledged, aside from surveys, were social media networks, which only generated five responses or 18.5% of responses. In regard to this survey, banking providers have not been successful in engaging or informing their customers about the CSR activities, events, or important changes within their organization. When participants were questioned about their familiarity with the monthly debit fee from various banking providers, 27% (n=23) of respondents were not aware of the potential charge, and 56% of respondents did not approve of the amount of communication concerning the reasons behind the charge (n=55).

This lapse in the recognition of CSR activities presents a clear indication that organizations must improve their communication to reduce the numbers of respondents who are unaware of pertinent information. This research supports the need for new strategies that must be created in order to inform stakeholders of an organization's CSR activities (Luo & Bhattacharya, 2006). When organizations fail to communicate major issues, the chance for an organization to influence support toward

their social initiatives significantly decreases (Luo &
Bhattacharya, 2006).

The third research question produced surprising
results behind the reasons a customer may associate with a
services from an organization, based on their CSR activity.
The banking provider with the most customers in this
survey was Bank of America (n=31), and 46.8% of
participants were affiliated with one of "The Big Five"
banking providers (Bank of America, Wells Fargo, Chase,
SunTrust Banks, Regents Bank) (n=40). Most, 97.6
percent, of the participants already had a banking provider
(n=81), prior to completing the survey. It should be noted
that SunTrust Banks and Regions banks had zero
customers participating in this study, despite being a
major bank mentioned. The bulk of respondents were
affiliated with smaller, local banks such as Peoples United
Bank (n=6), or a member of a credit union (n=11).
Participants in the study also appear to be "typical"
bankers, utilizing basic services offered, with checking
accounts (n=82), savings accounts (n=76), debit/credit
cards (n=73) and loan services (n=33) as the top four
reasons for association.

One of the more surprising outcomes from this study
was centered upon college as a tool for bank association.
The majority of respondents had already completed college
(n=55) or were currently enrolled (n=20). Thirty-four
percent of participants signed up for their banking
provider while in college (n=28), and are still enrolled as
customers. This study reflects earlier work from
Ledingham (2003), who recognized the importance of a
company's strategic positioning among their target
population in order to manage the relationship between
organization and customer. These results provide a large
amount of support toward convenience and location

playing a large role in the possible reasons a customer might associate with an organization.

Contact between individuals and banking providers did not play the large role that was expected in organization approval, in terms of perceived reputation. A correlation did exist between gender and support or lack of approval of the proposed debit card usage fee. Ironically, there was no association between gender and awareness of the proposed debit fee. The information regarding contact, while helpful, was not a major contributor establishing higher ratings of approval.

Hypotheses

It was rewarding to see numerous points of significance between the presence of customer's overall satisfaction and credibility (which was composed of goodwill, competence, and trust) in H1. Participants appear to be satisfied when their bank is seen as a credible source. Additionally, competence, overall satisfaction, and accessibility were rated high when banking providers catered to customer needs, and offered convenient services. This finding supports the development of CRM based relationships through positive customer experiences. The organizations that create comfortable and friendly environments have the ability to influence a customer's satisfaction beyond their initial expectations (Reimann et al, 2010). The connection between convenience and accessibility also suggests that CRM usage was most likely included as a managerial priority. The organizations that are considered accessible often oversee and manage their own CRM channels in order make sure their communication outlets remain available for customer involvement (Reinartz et al, 2004).

An organization's reputation was powerfully associated with an individuals' overall satisfaction, supporting H2, and this study as a whole. The importance of positive perceptions through PR campaigns, marketing tactics, or CRM channels explored in this study, provide tremendous evidence to support OP relationships as means to improve customer satisfaction and increase retention. People give positive evaluations about the organizations they are affiliated with, because our personal associations help to create our perceptions of self-identification (Fiske, 2010). Individuals like to create positive attitudes about their decisions (Fiske, 2010), which suggests that participants who were satisfied gave score higher ratings of a positive reputation.

The bridge between CRM and Public Relations was also enhanced from H3. An individual's reason to identify with their banking provider was not only tied to the reputation of the organization, but whether or not the customer's experience appeared to be inclusive. Participants felt supported by the banking providers who recognized their patronage, which in return, made customers feel involved. Those feelings of involvement lead to positive reputations for a bank, and induced feelings of familiarity between the customers and the company. For PR practitioners and their organizations, this relationship must be evident for all companies that wish to create various levels of identification and assimilation through their OP relationships (Bruning & Ledingham, 1998). Role negotiation also had a correlation with the amount times participants contacted their bank, suggesting that those individuals who were invested and identified with their bank had higher rates of communication. If an action is performed consistently, past behaviors are often considered to be strong indicators of predicting future behavior behaviors (Ajzen, 2002).

Limitations

While there was an incredible amount of support in favor of CRM programs as a function of Public Relations, several limitations should be noted. Due to participants withdrawing throughout the questionnaire, there were an inconsistent number of completed surveys, which resulted in various sections having higher or lower (n) scores. This was most likely caused by the distribution process of the survey, which was completely administered online. Perhaps, if tangible hard-copies were given out in conjunction with online solicitation, the overall number of participants might be higher and more consistent.

This study was conducted using a non-random snowball sampling campaign in order to create the participant pool. While this was convenient for the study and for the researcher, this process lacks the true sporadic distribution needed to create a sample representative of all members from the population. The study did an excellent job at attaining diversity among participants, but there was a noticeably large difference in the number of male-to-female participants. This inequity has most likely influenced the possibility of a 'gender effect' among the results of the study. With only 23 participants who identified as male participants, the responses might be skewed toward the answers provided from the noticeably large female presence.

Another limitation that may have deterred participants was the length of the survey. The time commitment was around 10 minutes, and participants were asked 86 questions. Even though the majority of participants answered 100% of questions asked, the study received a fair percentage of incomplete responses. More questions regarding the actual PR perceptions of an organization, and the opportunity for participants to respond with open-ended answers, might have provided the researcher with in depth analysis of the association between PR and particular CRM tools.

Future Research

Future direction for research should focus upon which CRM channels are preferred by PR practitioners when addressing organizational stakeholders, and how participants rate the representative who is providing the message. This would be an interesting study, due to the high preference for direct representatives when communicating with an organization. Participants could listen to a speech or watch a video and then evaluate the individual's performance based on a TARES test, discussed in Bakers and Martinson's *Out of the Red-Light District: Five Principles for Ethically Proactive Public Relations* (2002). Ratings would be based on The Truthfulness, Authenticity, Respect, Equity, and Social Responsibility of both the message and the representative. This process would allow researchers to assess participant reactions of both the message provided to the audience, as well as the individual who is affiliated.

Another avenue of research would be to repeat the same test, but re-evaluate the role of demographics and segmentation. Renewed concentration should be given to recognizing the ages of individuals who associate with a particular organization, whether or not the organization is regionally, nationally, or globally operated, or if the income or class status of an individual will influence the amount of significance given to developing OP relationships. Using an actual CRM program to retrieve results would also provide an opportunity for researchers to assess how effective CRM programming can be first-hand. Though the CSR portion of this study was not explored to its full potential, the topic is still relevant to PR practitioners and organizational identification. Researchers should consider the ways specific CSR activities (such as philanthropic contributions or research and development activities) can support organizational assimilation by identifying which activities will improve the organization's reputation and increase customers' overall satisfaction. Finally, researchers should focus directly on face-to-face CRM experiences in order to attain a better understanding of the CRM-PR relationship. Focus groups that include literature/examples of material from organizations could be used to compare and contrast organizations as a way to evaluate customer loyalty, satisfaction and retention.

CHAPTER V

As society increases its comprehension of Customer Relationship Management, the attention is now placed on the ways an organization can incorporate current trends in technology through constant communication efforts, consistency in their message, and compatibility with all forms of media. The opportunities to connect with customers continuously increases with each technological "boom", leading us far from the initial days of simple sales representatives and telephone calls to solicit contact with stakeholders. With such vast leaps in innovation, consideration for "cloud" based programming, mobile involvement, and the inclusion social media services and networks that work alongside the traditional CRM practices, companies can offer more comprehensive CRM package in several ways.

Research from Fragouli & Noutrixa (2014) cite several authors who have studied current technological trends CRM who show considerable support toward its impact upon in any organization. In 2001 it was estimated 45% of companies using some form of CRM programming (as cited by Leon, 2001), and with over a decade of new tools, programs, and applications to support customer interaction, organizations now have choices in their CRM services. Shopping for CRM programs can include features such as community based open sourced programming, increased mobile device activity, website data tracking to monitor individual purchasing habits and activity (Fragouli & Noutrixa, 2014), and in many cases, unlimited access to remote assistance from outsourced third party companies to alleviate the need for permanent office space.

Selecting the right program can be a very difficult task, due to an oversaturated market filled with thousands of applications available for companies of all shapes and sizes, who search and seek for the 'holy grail' of customer communication. CRM platforms can vary from free services for small enterprises, to very specific rates for and bundled subscriptions on an annual basis. Companies such as Merrill Lynch take advance of these potential savings, having reduced part of their software expense budget by incorporating open sourced CRM programs with their customer service activities (Stoddard, 2009). This expansion of CRM programming provides unique software packages and price points, driving competition between competitors but also forcing companies to distinguish themselves from one another. In return, the focus of CRM and Public Relations can search beyond deciding which tools are best associated with reaching and engaging stakeholders, but also determine which companies are able to deliver truly innovative means of supporting the customer life cycle beyond the initial purchase.

The inclusion of Cloud Based Programming (CBP) is a recurring theme throughout the latest trends CRM, allowing both the customer and the company to maintain consistent communication. Cloud based CRM not only transmits information to be reached by anyone who is connected to the internet (Rodriguez, M., & Honeycutt, 2011) but it also offers the addition of a mobile component, which has become a prominent role in reinforcing open channels of communication desired by OP relationships. The role of social media is also highlighted as a fast growing trend for CRM programmers due to the consistent activity from users and the opportunity to gather both empirical and emotional responds from potential stakeholders. Working in tandem, each company must have the ability to include these features when creating specific CRM applications to boost involvement with a particular type of software. When a company can successfully incorporate the majority, if not all of these modern trends of CRM, their ability to maintain a strong OP relationship can increase; more important however, is their opportunity to project a consistent image of accessibility and interconnectivity that can play a decisive role in maintaining a positive public perception.

CRM and the Cloud
As mentioned before, the expansive list of tools and programs under the umbrella of Customer Relationship Management can be overwhelming. With options that vary from soliciting potential customers at kiosks, to text message invitations for interactive webcam sessions, the advent of eCRM activity is consistently reinventing itself to match the demands of the public. This concept of continued evolution in a specific technology is derived from Everett Roger's *Diffusion of Innovations* (1962, as cited by Rodriguez, M., & Honeycutt, 2011), a theory that explores that relationship between the use of a new technology and its ability to determine the growth of that technology over a specific time span and across cultures (p.336). Similar to CRM support, there is a growing need to not only store massive collections of consumer information, but new responsibilities includes monitoring the most effective ways to *retrieve* data, and best methods available to transform data into future touch points.

Using the "cloud" as a form of computer processing allows the internet to serve as the medium between any accessible parties and content from another (Sosa-Sosa & Hernandez-Ramirez, 2012). Sosa-Sosa & Hernandez-Ramirez (2012) expand this definition of the cloud, stating:

A cloud environment provides omnipresence and facilitates deployment of file-storage services. It means that users can access their files via the Internet from anywhere and without requiring the installation of a special application. The user only needs a web browser (Sosa-Sosa & Hernandez-Ramirez, 2012 (p.35).

Cloud Based Programming (CBP) offers individuals and organizations immediate retrieval to personal data, (ex. text documents, music and videos, and other miscellaneous files), while providing companies with the ability to secure entire libraries of information via virtual content storage. CBP services vary in similar ways to CRM programs: they are used by the general public, private organizations, and mixtures of both populations (ex. College campuses where both students and professionals use the same system), with some cloud services offered through open source models and others with premium subscription fees (Sosa-Sosa & Hernandez-Ramirez, 2012).

The connection between CRM and CBP has become so intertwined that companies are saving significant amounts of dollars in distribution fees while others generate new revenue with premium content services. Because each company has its own specific attributes to encourage association, there are typically various levels of cloud integration. If using an open source CBP, the benefits considered typically include minimal initiation and set up of programs, along with strong community involvement with programmers; when many people use the same program, problems are usually easier to monitor, increased maintenance is available, and free/low cost options are usually easier to find (Klie, 2012).

When using premium services, integration across programs and visual platforms are known for smooth transitions between each interfaces (Rodriguez & Honeycutt, 2011). Programs such as Microsoft Dynamics CRM and Salesforce.com offer distinct options in their software packages, providing the choice between direct installations on company machines, access to their files on the cloud, or both locations (Rodriguez & Honeycutt, 2011). Subscription based CRM programs often have the same features of open sourced CBPs, plus added benefits of 24/7 assistance, increased user capabilities, and several options to upgrade. Regardless of price point, the added benefit of cloud programming is to ensure successful operation of the service beyond the traditional accessibility of past CRM models.

CRM Tools:
Mobile Access and Social Media Integration

With the worldwide interconnected atmosphere created by the cloud, CRM programs and their initiatives to support customer contact and satisfaction have advanced to the point where any individual with a mobile device has a direct line of communication to an organization. The progression of mobileCRM (mCRM) is inspired by individuals who are on the go, but are still involved with an organization by way of shopping, completing surveys, and texting/calling organizations, or when necessary, commutating complaints, or suggestions to improve customer service (Lee & Engelman, 2012). mCRM is an increasing trend among retail companies, with their customer retention goals influenced by frequent shoppers who have a stronger connection to an organization due to brand loyalty (as cited by Chan and Lam, 2004). The majority of the big names in CRM development have at least one form of mobile connectivity, whether it is creating a series of applications built for Smartphone usage, or at the minimum, basic applications that transform their main website into a reduced and navigable interface for viewing on a mobile device.

A Social media network is a website created to provide individuals and organizations the opportunity to share personal information, including demographic content, expressions, and personal opinions, all while building relationships with others through a personalized interconnected network (Wang, Dugan, and Sojka, 2013). Social networks such as Facebook, Linkedin, Twitter and others have the largest volumes of activity and their data (traffic) is often measured similar to that of traditional CRM channels. At the time of research, Wang et. al (2014) noted that over 845 million users were registered on Facebook, (as cited by Henschen, 2012), which has steadily increased over the years. This volume of activity from one website alone supports the notion of CRM and social media integration.

Conversations in Communication ®
Volume II

Customer Relationship Management (CRM) as a Function of Public Relations

FUNDING FOR CRM:

2.8 Billion (1998) to 16.8 Billion (2003) to
20.4 Billion (2013)
(update via forbes.com).

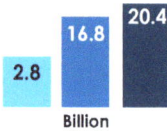

20.4
16.8
2.8
Billion

FIVE MOST POPULAR PROGRAMS:

Salesforce.com/OracleCRM
Microsoft Dynamics/ SAP
Crm/SugarCRM/ZohoCRM.

salesforce | ORACLE
SAP | ZOHO

Elliot's (2001) research measures company investments in CRM funding from the early mid-to-late 1990's to mid 2000's, and found that CRM industry sales increased from $2.8billion in 1998, to projections of over $16.8 billion
in 2003 (p. 49).

In 2005, there were five major CRM programs mentioned in the Statistically Speaking **(2006)** column pertaining to CRM growth and product market share.

The top five organizations generated nearly $3.5billion alone, with SAP (Systems Analysis and Program Development) generating over $1.4 billion, Siebel systems with $966 million, and Oracle with $367 million. The CRM programs offered from Salesforce.com and Amdocs rounded out the top five with $280 million, and with $276 million, respectively
(Statistically Speaking, 2006, p. 16). " -Jabaree Dunham-Carson

SAP :over $1.4 billion   salesforce :$280 million

SIEBEL :$966 million

ORACLE :367 million

Not only has social networks become an important CRM tool that can determine the effectiveness of a particular program, but the demand to include social networks as a medium for outreach is also encouraged. When integrating social media and CRM, studies from Arman (2014) describe how important the connection between the two can be when deciding which software packages offer the best collaboration with social network websites. When companies use their CRM capabilities to connect with social media networks, there is a large return on the investment, with 72% of their participants intending to connect to their social networks through their CRM programs within a year (Arman, 2014, as cited by Blankenhorn, 2011). Social media has become one of the largest means of online communication, with more individuals who are associated with social networks than email users (Bruckenstein, 2012), in addition to over a billion users subscribed to some form of social media. This is a clear indication that in order to communicate with your target audience, the presence of CRM and social media much be displayed as a priority among the dominant coalition of any organization.

CRM Organization profiles

Having discussed the important roles of cloud access, mobile customer relationship management, and social media involvement, together these three components add to the success of a modern and influential CRM campaign. While some organizations are known for including these models of communication in their software, others stand out for their mastery of a certain application. In 2008, the CRM market was led by four companies who collectively held 55 percent control over distribution and implementation (Wang et al, 2013, as cited by Gartner, 2009). Of these companies, SalesForce.com and Microsoft Corporation are known for their total inclusion of cloud, social media, and mobile based CRM applications. On the opposite end of the market, ZohoOfficeSuite and SugarCRM are influenced by both open source and privately managed CRM programs and specifically address organizational needs such as content management and outsourcing responsibilities to third party companies. Regardless of the organization, all provide potential users with the option of exploring their programs for free (either a basic level or trail period), in addition to premium services to support the best communication between stakeholders and the organization.

Salesforce

Website: http://www.salesforce.com/
Pricing Details: http://www.salesforce.com/crm/ editions-pricing-flyout.jsp

Created in 1999, Salesforce.com is a cloud based, multi-billion dollar organization that focuses on the growth and development of all aspects within an organization. Serving over 100,000 customers who produce billions of transactions (Bruckenstein, 2012), Salesforce.com has mastered CRM communication by focusing on three areas of growth: Sale, Service, and Customization. When tracking data with Salesforce.com, their "sales" cloud includes traditional CRM management (trends/growth in population, search engine optimization, IT management) while their social media involvement is managed through their "service" cloud which allows users to monitor both in house communication (ex. their instant messaging "chatter" platform (p.66) and external communication with customers by engaging directly via social media involvement (Bruckenstein, 2012). Through their "custom" cloud, over 200,000+ applications are available for organizations to support both internal and external IT maintenance. Salesforce.com applications vary from programs that can attach demographic information to incoming calls, to their "Radian6" platform, which allows companies to track what comments and posts are created by their clients by attaching their online responses to a managed system of user profiles (Bruckensetin, 2012, (p.67). Salesforce.com's entry CRM program is $5 a month per user (up to 5 users), ideal for smaller companies, while their unlimited edition (priced at $300 a month per user/month) includes unlimited global support, data cleansing and improved accessibility between departments and increased storage content.

Salesforce Screenshot #1

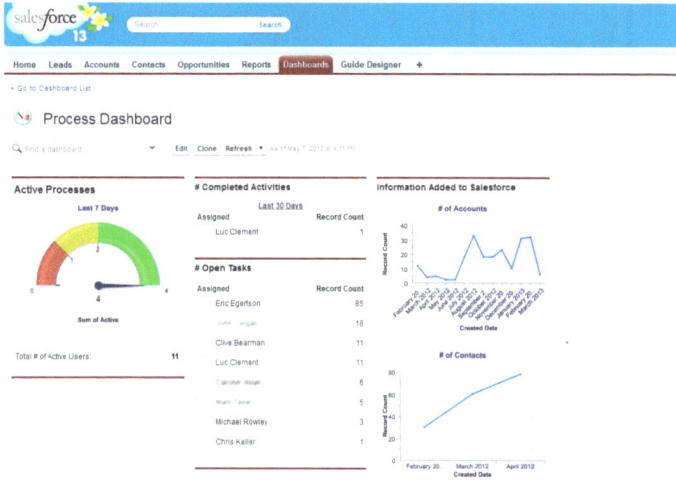

Retrieved from: https://community.informatica.com/servlet/JiveServlet/
showImage/38-1074-4647/reports.png

Salesforce Screenshot #2

Retrieved from: http://www.cirrusinsight.com/wp-content uploads/2014/06/
6a00e54ee3905b88330192ac45be1d970d.png

Zoho

Website: http://www.zoho.com/crm/
Pricing Details: https://www.zoho.com/crm/zohocrm-pricing.html

Overview: Zoho's entry level program is free for up to three users and includes the typical CRM programs (ex. lead management, language support, account and contact management, social media connections, and statistical analysis), all the way up to the Enterprise at $35 per user (unlimited) which has "territory management" to provide their clients with connections to outsourced call centers, and a 24-hour help desk.'

Retrieved from: http://static3.businessinsider.com/image/4ced55feccd1d5
ae1d0b0000-1200/zoho-is-an-affordable-crm-option.jpg

Zoho CRM Screenshot

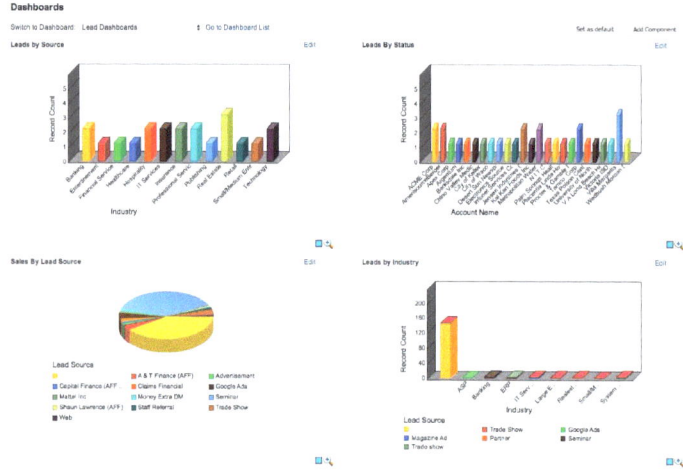

Retrieved from: https://www.zoho.com/crm/images/marketing-dashboard.png

Zoho CRM Screenshot #2

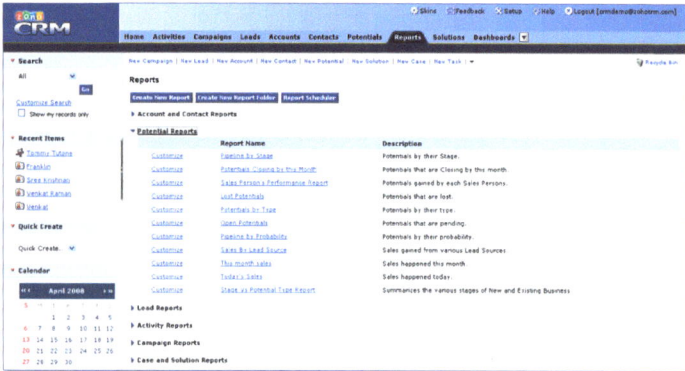

Retrieved from: https://www.zoho.com/crm/images/report.gif

SugarCRM

Website: http://www.sugarcrm.com/
Pricing Details: http://www.sugarcrm.com/pricing

Overview: SugarCRM's entry level package is "Sugar Professional" at $35 per user/month (annual bill) but a minimum of ten registered users is necessary (creating an annual fee of $4200). Traditional CRM features are included (market/support automation), in addition to mobile apps, cloud connectivity, and access to an "online product training and webcast." Unlimited support cases are available to the Sugar Ultimate user(s) for $150 per user/month (annual bill) which also includes 24/7 support, an assigned account manager, and increased storage and activity streams.

Customer Relationship Management (CRM) as a Function of Public Relations

SugarCRM Screen Shot 1

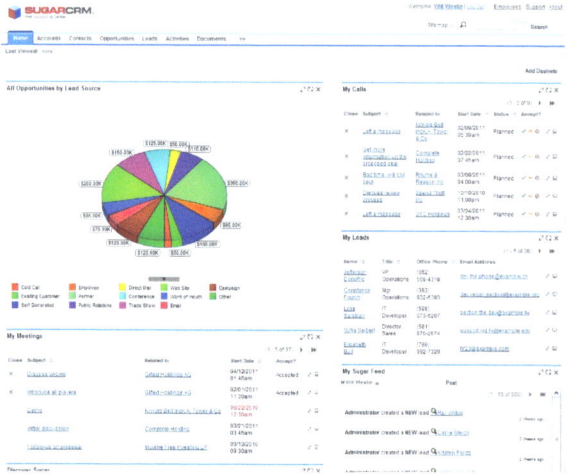

Retrieved from: http://www.sugarforge.org/screenshots/screenshot.php/6/1862/fullsize/Home-Dashboard.jpg

SugarCRM Screen Shot 2

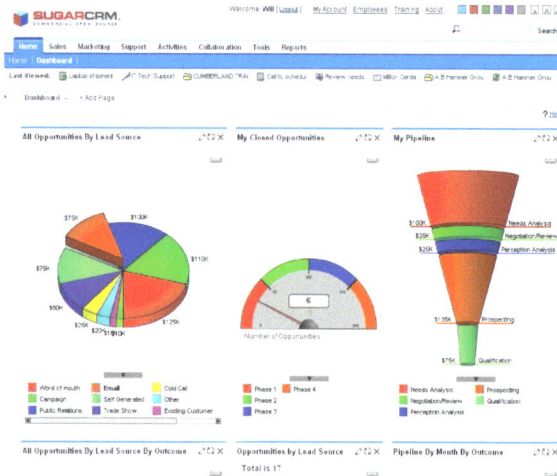

Retrieved from: http://www.crm-reviews.com/wp-content/uploads/2010/12/sugarcrm-dashboards-screen.jpg

Microsoft Dynamics

Website: http://www.microsoft.com/en-us/dynamics/
Pricing Details: http://www.microsoft.com/en-us/
dynamics/crm-purchase-online.aspx

Overview: Microsoft Dynamics offers three
communication platforms: Sales, Social, and Marketing.
The Sales/Social packages both start at $65 user/month
with features that include the traditional CRM tools. For
$100, companies can upgrade to their "Social listening and
analysis" program that includes social sentiment tracking
and trending alerts. Upgrade to the sales package under
the "Enterprise" label is $200 which includes increased
content management, brand development and inclusion of
their "Microsoft Dynamics Marketing package."

Appendix A: List of Acronyms

B2B:	Business-to-Business
B2C:	Business-to-Consumer
CLC:	Customer Life Cycle
CLV:	Customer Life Value
CRM:	Customer Relationship Management
CS:	Customer Share
CSR:	Corporate Social Responsibility
eCRM:	Electronic Customer Relationship Management
OP:	Organization-Public
PR:	Public Relations
RM:	Relationship Management
WOM:	Word-of-Mouth
OAI:	Organizational Assimilation Index

Appendix B: Demographic Figures and Tables

Table 1 A-D
Demographic Information

(A)

Gender	Response Percent	Frequency (n)
Male	27.4%	23
Female	72.6%	61

n=84

(B)

Ethnicity	Response Percent	Frequency (n)
African American/Black	22.1%	22
Asian/Pacific Islander	2.4%	2
Caucasian/White	60.7%	51
Latino/Hispanic	2.4%	2
Multi-Racial (2+ Backgrounds)	3.6%	3
Other	3.6%	3
Preferred not to respond	1.2%	1

n=84

(C)

College Attendance	Response Percent	Frequency (n)
Yes-Graduated	65.5%	55
Yes-Currently Enrolled	23.8%	20
No-Not enrolled/did not complete	10.7%	9

n=84

(D)

Income Range	Response Percent	Frequency (n)
$0-19,999	28.0%	23
$20,000-39,999	29.3%	24
$40,000-59,999	19.6%	16
$60,000-79,999	8.6%	7
$80,000-99,999	2.4%	2
$100,000+	6.1%	5
Prefer not to respond	6.1%	5

n=83

Appendix C: Research Scales

To recall from Chapter IV, there were four scales of measurement used to evaluate the relationship between Customer Relationship Management and Public Relations. Each scale focused on a major aspect of CRM or PR, and the overall range of measurement from these surveys collectively covered the impact of organizational influence, reputation, customer assimilation, customer satisfaction, and credibility.

The scales are included for future researchers who wish to continue exploring and discovering future relationships between customers, organizations, and the communication that occurs between the two. All scales, with the exception of the Dunham-Carson scale, can be found in *Communication Research Measures II: A Soucebook(2009)* with author and editor information located in the references section. Note that slight modifications were made to the scales used for this study; please refer back to Chapter IV for more information regarding the changes made during research.

Customer Relationships and Banking Services

Dunham-Carson, 2010

Thank you for your participation in this survey. Please take time to answer each of the following questions. Please be honest in your answers, as all surveys are anonymous and there is no right or wrong response. When the survey has been completed please be sure to exit your browser.

1) **Sex**:
   ____Male   ____Female

   Age:
   ____18-24 ____25-29 ____30-35 ____ 36-40 ____ 41+

2) **Ethnicity:**
   ____African American/Black   ____Middle Eastern

   ____Asian/Pacific Islander   ____Multi-Racial

   ____White/Caucasian   ____Other (_____)

   ____Latino/Hispanic   ____Prefer not to answer

3) **Did you attend college/are you currently in college?**

   ____Yes (Graduated)   ____Yes (Currently Enrolled)   ____No (I am not in college/did not complete)

4) **Do you currently have a checking/savings account? (If yes, please skip to Question 6)**
   ____Yes   ____No

5) **If not, do intend to create one in the next 6 months?**
   ____Yes   ____No

6) **Did you sign up with a bank while enrolled in college?**
   ____Yes   ____No

   If so, are you still enrolled in your college banking services?

   ____Yes   ____No

7) **Do you have more than one (1) checking/savings account?**
   ____Yes   ____No

If so, how many banking accounts do you have (in total)?

_____

8) **How would you rate your current banking experience in terms of satisfaction?**
____Excellent ____Good ____Acceptable ____Bad ____Poor

9) **Do you plan on closing your account with your banking provider(s) within the next 6 months?**
____Yes ____No ____I do not have a banking account

10) **Do you currently have a checking account with the following banks? (Check all that apply)**
____Bank of America ____Wells Fargo ____Chase
____SunTrust Banks ____Regions Bank ____I do not have any of these banking providers

If not, who is your primary banking provider (the bank you use the most)?
_____ ____I do not have a checking account

11) **Have you received any notice of information regarding fees, interest rates, minimum balances, etc., from your primary bank in the past 6 months?**
_____Yes _____No _____I do not have a checking account

If so, how many times were you contacted within the past 6 months?

____1-2 times ____2-3 times ____3-4 times ____4-5 times
____6+ times

12) **Were you aware of the attempted monthly debit card usage fee (an additional $3-5 dollars depending on bank) that would be charged to customers?**
____Yes ____No

13) **How much would you agree that the banking providers (listed in question 8) effectively communicated the reasons behind the possible increase in fees?**
____Strongly Agree ____Agree ____Disagree
____Strongly Disagree ____I was not aware of the additional banking fees

14) **Were you in support of this increase in service fees?**
____Yes ____No ____Did not mind

15) **How often do you contact your banking provider each year?**
___0 times ___1-2 times ___3-4 times ___5-6 times ___7+ times ___I do not have a banking provider

16) **What is your preferred form of communication with your banking provider? Please rank your choices from 1-5 (1 being the most preferred through 5 being the lease preferred)**
__Speaking with Customer Representatives/Automated (ATM/Kiosks)
__Emails __Direct Mailings __Online Banking Transactions
__Mobile/Tablet applications

17) **Do you participant any of the following activities sponsored by your banking provider(s)? (Check all that apply)**
__Surveys/Questionnaires
__Social media networks (Facebook, Twitter, YouTube, etc.)
__ Community Events (festivals, marathons, benefit events, etc.)
__Organizational Newsletters
__Other (please specify) _____

18) **What is your current yearly income?**
___$0-9,999 ___$10,000-19,999 ___$20,000-29,999
___$30,000-39,999 ___$40,000-49,999 ___$50,000, 59,999
___$60,000-69,999 ___$70,000-79,999 ___$80,000-89,999
___$90,999-99,999 ___$100,000+ ___I prefer not to respond

19) **What banking services do you utilize? (check all that apply)**
___Checking account ___Savings account ___Money market account
___Money orders ___Traveler's checks
___Credit/Debit Cards
___Foreign currency ___Loans (auto, home, business, etc.)
___Other (_____

Organizational Reputation Scale

McCroskey, 1996; α =.81-.92

Instructions: The items below concern your impression of your **primary banking provider**. Circle one number for each of the questions. The response ranges from 1=STRONGLY DISAGREE to 5=STRONGLY AGREE.

1. My Banking service is basically honest

   STRONGLY DISAGREE   STRONGLY AGREE

   1   2   3   4   5

2. The organization is concerned with the well-being of its publics.

   STRONGLY DISAGREE   STRONGLY AGREE

   1   2   3   4   5

3. I do trust the organization to tell the truth about any incidents.

   STRONGLY DISAGREE   STRONGLY AGREE

   1   2   3   4   5

4. I would prefer to have NOTHING to do with this organization.

   STRONGLY DISAGREE   STRONGLY AGREE

   1   2   3   4   5

5. Under most circumstances, I WOULD NOT be likely to believe what the organization says.

   STRONGLY DISAGREE   STRONGLY AGREE

   1   2   3   4   5

6. The organization is basically DISHONEST.

   STRONGLY DISAGREE   STRONGLY AGREE

   1   2   3   4   5

7. I do NOT trust the organization to tell the truth about any incidents.

   STRONGLY DISAGREE   STRONGLY AGREE

   1   2   3   4   5

8. Under most circumstances, I would be likely to believe what the organization says.

   STRONGLY DISAGREE   STRONGLY AGREE

   1   2   3   4   5

9. I would continue service with this organization

   STRONGLY DISAGREE   STRONGLY AGREE

   1   2   3   4   5

10. The organization is NOT concerned with the well-being of its publics.

    STRONGLY DISAGREE   STRONGLY AGREE

    1   2   3   4   5

Organizational Assimilation Index (OAI)

Myers & Oetzel, 2003; α =.62-.86

Instructions: Please respond to a series of questions about being a customer to an organization. For this research, organization refers to your affiliation with your primary banking provider. There is no right or wrong answers in this survey; I simply want to know what you think about and feel about your organization. REMEMBER, YOUR ANSWERS WILL REMAIN CONFIDENTIAL. YOUR BANKING PROVIDER WILL NOT SEE YOUR RESPONSES TO THE QUESTIONS. For each question, please circle your response according to the following scale:

Strongly Disagree	Disagree	Neutral	Agree	Strongly Agree
1	2	3	4	5

Familiarity

I feel like I know my banking provider pretty well	1 2 3 4 5
My bank contacts me regarding organizational issues	1 2 3 4 5
My bank and I communicate often	1 2 3 4 5

Acculturation

I understand the standards of the company	1 2 3 4 5
I think I have a good idea about how this organization operates	1 2 3 4 5
I know the values associated with my bank	1 2 3 4 5

Recognition

My bank recognizes my commitment	1 2 3 4 5
My bank listens to my suggestions	1 2 3 4 5
I think my bank values my opinions	1 2 3 4 5
I think my bank recognizes my value to the organization	1 2 3 4 5

Involvement

I talk to my friends about how much I like my bank(s)	1 2 3 4 5
I voluntarily recommend the bank's services to benefit the organization	1 2 3 4 5
I talk about how much I enjoy my banking services	1 2 3 4 5
I feel involved in the organization	1 2 3 4 5

Role Negotiation

I have offered suggestions for how to improve productivity	1 2 3 4 5

Measure of Source Credibility

Teven & McCroskey, 1997; α =.94

Instructions: Please indicate your impressions of the banking provider to
which you are primarily affiliated, by circling the appropriate number between
the pairs of adjectives below. The closer the number is to an adjective, the
more certain you are of your evaluation.

Competence

1.	Intelligent	1 2 3 4 5 6 7	Unintelligent (R)
2.	Untrained	1 2 3 4 5 6 7	Trained
3.	Inexperienced organization	1 2 3 4 5 6 7	Experienced organization
4.	Informed	1 2 3 4 5 6 7	Uninformed (R)
5.	Incompetent	1 2 3 4 5 6 7	Competent
6.	Bright	1 2 3 4 5 6 7	Stupid (R)

Goodwill

7.	cares about me	1 2 3 4 5 6 7	Doesn't care about me (R)
8.	Has my interest at heart	1 2 3 4 5 6 7	Doesn't have my interest at heart (R)
9.	Self-concerned	1 2 3 4 5 6 7	Not self-concerned
10.	Concerned with me	1 2 3 4 5 6 7	Not concerned with me (R)
11.	Insensitive	1 2 3 4 5 6 7	Sensitive
12.	Not understanding	1 2 3 4 5 6 7	Understanding

Trustworthiness

13.	Honest	1 2 3 4 5 6 7	Dishonest (R)
14.	Untrustworthy	1 2 3 4 5 6 7	Trustworthy
15.	Honorable	1 2 3 4 5 6 7	Dishonorable (R)
16.	Moral	1 2 3 4 5 6 7	Immoral (R)
17.	Unethical	1 2 3 4 5 6 7	Ethical
18.	Phony	1 2 3 4 5 6 7	Genuine

References

Ajzen, I. (2002). Residual effects of past on later behavior: Habituation and reasoned action
perspectives. *Personality & Social Psychology Review, 6*(2), 107-122.

Ajzen, I. (1991). The theory of planned behavior. *Organizational Behavior and Human
Decision Processes, 50,* 179-211

Ajzen, I., & Driver, B.L. (1992). Application of the theory of planned behavior to leisure
choice. (1992). *Journal of Leisure Research, 24*(3), 207.

Ajzen, I., & Driver, B. L. (1992). Contingent value measurement: On the nature
and meaning of willingness to pay. *Journal of Consumer Psychology, 1,* 297-316.

Arman, S. d. (2014). Integrated model of Social Media and Customer Relationship Management:
A Literature Review.International Journal Of Information, Business & Management,6(3),
118-131.

Aurier, P., & N'Goala, G. (2010). The differing and mediating roles of trust and
relationship commitment in service relationship maintenance and development. *Journal
of the Academy of Marketing Science, 38*(3), 303-325.

Baker, S., & Martinson, D. L. (2002). Out of the Red-Light district: Five principles for   ethically
proactive public relations. *Public Relations Quarterly, 47*(3), 15.

Bansal H., & Taylor S. (2002) Investigating interactive effects in the theory of planned
behavior in a service-provider switching context. *Psychology & Marketing,*
May 2002 *19*(5), 407-425.

Bauer, R. (1960). Consumer behavior as risk taking. *Proceedings, American Market
Association* pp. 389-398

Bell, S. J., Auh, S., & Smalley, K. (2005). Customer relationship dynamics: service
quality and customer loyalty in the context of varying levels of customer expertise and
switching costs. *Journal of the Academy of Marketing Science, 33*(2), 169-183.

Berner, R. (2005). Smarter corporate giving. *Business-Week,* (November 28), 68–76.

Bhattacharya, C. B., & Elsbach, K. D. (2002). Us versus them: The roles of
organizational identification and disidentification in social marketing initiatives. *Journal
of Public Policy & Marketing, 21,* 26–36.

Blankenhorn, D (2011), Firms Integrating Social Media With CRM. *InformationWeek* January
21, 2011, Retrieved from

Customer Relationship Management (CRM) as a Function of Public Relations

http://www.informationweek.com/news/software/productivity_apps/229100015

Blattberg, R. C., Getz, G., & Thomas, J. S. (2001). Customer equity: Building and managing relationships as valuable assets. Boston: Harvard Business School.

Boulding, W., Staelin, R., Ehret, M., & Johnston, W. J. (2005). A customer relationship management roadmap: What is known, potential pitfalls, and where to go. *Journal of Marketing*, 69(4), 155-166. doi:10.1509/jmkg.2005.69.4.155

Brønn, P. (2008). Why aren't we measuring relationships? *Communication World*, 25(1), 32-34

Brandon, J. (2009). Track your customers with free CRM tools. *Inc, 31*(8), 48.

Bruckenstein, J. (2012). Salesforce: More than Just CRM. *Financial Planning, 42*(1), 65-67.

Bruning, S. D., & Ledingham, J. A. (1998). Organization-public relationships and consumer satisfaction: The role of relationships in the satisfaction mix. *Communication Research Reports, 15*(2), 198-208.

Bruning, S. D. (2001). Axioms of relationship management: Applying interpersonal communication principles to the public relations context. *Journal of Promotion Management,* 7(1/2), 3.

Cardwell, J. (1997). Career paths in public relations. In C. L. Caywood, ed., *The Handbook of Strategic Public Relations and Integrated Communications*. New York: McGraw-Hill, 3-14.

Chan, S., & Lam, J. (2004). Customer Relationship Management on Internet and Mobile Channels: An Analytical Framework and Research Directions .In P.Candace Deans (Eds.), *E--Commerc eand M--Commerce Technologies* (pp.2-20) .Hershey,PA :IRMPress.

Chao, Y., Chu, P.-Y., & Lee, G.-Y. (2011). Service quality, relationship quality, and customer loyalty in Taiwanese Internet banks. *Social Behavior and Personality: An International Journal, 39*(8), 1127+.

Cutlip, S. M., Center, A. H., and Broom, G. M. (1985). *Effective Public Relations*, 6th ed. Englewood Cliffs, NJ: Prentice Hall.

Coombs, W.T., & Holladay, S.J. (1996). Communication and attributions in a crisis: An experimental study of crisis communication. *Journal of Public Relations Research, 8,*279 295.

Day, G. S. (2004), "Invited Commentaries on 'Evolving to a New Dominant Logic for Marketing,'" *Journal of Marketing, 68* (1), 18–27.

Elliott, M. (2000). Customer relationship management software. *IIE Solutions, 32*(11), 44.

Customer Relationship Management (CRM) as a Function of Public Relations

Fiske, S. (2010). *Social Beings: Core Motives in Social Psychology*. Hoboken, NJ: John Wiley & Sons, Inc.

Fletcher, K. (2003). Consumer power and privacy: The changing nature of CRM. *International Journal of Advertising, 22*(2), 249-272.

Fragouli, E. E., & Noutrixa, A. A. (2014). Application of Electronic Customer Relationship Management (e-CRM) for promoting products and Services in a Local Context: Exploration of a Case. *International Journal Of Information, Business & Management,6*(4), 11-25.

Gartner Group. (2003). CRM success is in strategy and implementation, not software. Retrieved from http://www.gartner.com.

Gartner (2009), "Gartner Says Worldwide CRM Market Grew 12.5 Percent in 2008," Stamford, CT, July 15 (retrived from www.gartner.com/newsroom/id/1074615/).

Gronstedt, A. (1997). The role of research in public relations strategy and planning. In C. L. Caywood, ed., *The Handbook of Strategic Public Relations and Integrated Communications*. New York: McGraw-Hill, 34-59.

Grunig, J. E. (2006). Furnishing the edifice: Ongoing research on public relations as a strategic management function. *Journal of Public Relations Research, 18*(2), 151-176.

Grunig, J. E., & Grunig, L. (1989). Toward a theory of the public relations behavior of organizations: Review of a program of research. *Public Relations Research Annual, 127.*

Hall, M. R. (2006). Corporate philanthropy and corporate community relations: Measuring relationship-building results. *Journal of Public Relations Research, 18*(1), 1-21.

Henschen, Doug (2012), "How to Get from CRM to Social," *InformationWeek,* February 22 (available at www.informationweek.com/software/enterprise-applications/how-to-get-fromcrm-tosocial/232600963?ct=1022/).

Homburg, C., Hoyer, W. D., & Stock, R. (2007). How to get lost customers back? *Journal of the Academy of Marketing Science, 35*(4), 461-474.

Hong, S., & Yang, S. (2009). Effects of reputation, relational satisfaction, and customer- company identification on positive word-of-mouth intentions. *Journal of Public Relations Research, 21*(4), 381-403.

Horn, D., Feinberg, R., & Salvendy, G. (2005). Determinant elements of customer relationship management in e-business. *Behaviour & Information Technology, 24*(2), 101-109.

Customer Relationship Management (CRM) as a Function of Public Relations

Ihlen, Ø. (2010). Love in tough times: Crisis communication and public relations. *Review of Communication*, *10*(2), 98-111.

Jayachandran, S., Sharma, S., Kaufman, P., & Raman, P. (2005). The role of relational information processes and technology use in customer relationship management. *Journal of Marketing*, *69*(4), 177-192.

Kale, S. (2005). Change management: Antecedents and consequences in casino CRM. *UNLV Gaming Research & Review Journal*, *9*(2), 55-67.

Khalifa, M., and K. N. Shen. 2009. "Modeling electronic customer relationship management success: Functional and temporal considerations." *Behaviour & Information Technology* 28, no. 4: 373-387.*PsycINFO*, (accessed October 10, 2011).

Klie, L. (2012). OPEN-SOURCE CRM. *CRM Magazine*, *46*.

Kotler, P., & Lee, N., (2004). *Corporate social responsibility: Doing the most good for your company and your cause*. New York: John Wiley & Sons.

Krasnikov, A., Jayachandran, S., & Kumar, V. (2009). The Impact of Customer Relationship Management Implementation on Cost and Profit Efficiencies: Evidence from the U.S. Commercial Banking Industry. *Journal Of Marketing*, *73*(6), 61-76.

Ledingham, J. A. (2003). Explicating relationship management as a general theory of public relations. *Journal of Public Relations Research*, *15*(2), 181-198.

Lee, D., & Engelman, K. (2012). The Impact of Mobile on CPG CRM Strategy: A Kraft Canada Study. *International Journal of Mobile Marketing*, *7*(1), 5-22.

Lemon, K. N., White, T., & Winer, R. S. (2002). Dynamic customer relationship management: Incorporating future considerations into the service retention decision. *Journal of Marketing*, *66*(1), 1-14.

Leon, M. (2001), "CRM", InfoWorld, 17 July, pp.34-37, available at: http://www.emerald-library.com/ft

Lichtenstein, D. R., Drumwright, M.E., and Braig, B.M., (2004), "The effect of corporate social responsibility on customer donations to corporate-supported nonprofits," *Journal of Marketing*, *68* (October), 16–32.

Lindenmann, W. K. (1998). Measuring relationships is key to successful public relations. *Public Relations Quarterly*, *43*(4), 18-24.

Luo, X., & Bhattacharya, C. (2006). Corporate social responsibility, customer satisfaction, and market value. *Journal of Marketing*, *70*(4), 1-18.

Customer Relationship Management (CRM) as a Function of Public Relations

Marshall, D. (2005). Food as ritual, routine or convention. *Consumption, Markets & Culture, 8*(1), 69-85.

McCroskey, J.C. (1966). *An Introduction to Rhetorical Communication.* Englewood Cliffs, NJ: Prentice Hall.

McCroskey, J.C., Teven, J.J. (1999). Goodwill: A reexamination of the construct and its measurements. *Communication Monographs, 66,* 90-103.

Mithas, S., Krishnan, M. S., & Fornell, C. (2005). Why do customer relationship management applications affect customer satisfaction?. *Journal of Marketing, 69*(4), 201-209.

Musalem, A., & Joshi, Y. V. (2009). How much should you invest in each customer relationship? A competitive strategic approach. *Marketing Science, 28*(3), 555-565.

Myers, K.K., & Oetzel, J.G. (2003). Exploring the dimensions of organizational assimilation: Creating and validating a measure. *Communication Quarterly, 51* (4), 438-457.

Nakra, P. (2000). Corporate reputation management: "CRM" with a strategic twist?. *Public Relations Quarterly, 45*(2), 35-42.

No satisfaction for CRM users. (2002). *IIE Solutions, 34*(2),10.

Oliver, R. L., & Bearden, W. O. (1985). Crossover effects in the theory of reasoned action: A moderating influence attempt. *Journal of Consumer Research, 12*(3), 324-340. Peppers, Don and Martha Rogers (1997), *Enterprise One to One.* New York:Doubleday.

Ramaseshan, B., Bejou, D., Jain, S. C., Mason, C., & Pancras, J.(2006). Issues and perspectives in global customer relationship management. *Journal of Service Research, 9*(2), 195–207.

Reichheld, F.F., & Sasser, W.E., Jr. (1990). Zero defections: Quality comes to services. *Harvard Business Review, 68,* 105-111.

Reimann, M., Schilke, O., & Thomas, J. S. (2010). Customer relationship management and firm performance: The mediating role of business strategy. *Journal of the Academy of Marketing Science, 38*(3), 326-346.

Reinartz, W., Krafft, M., & Hoyer, W. D. (2004). The customer relationship management process: Its measurement and impact on performance. *Journal of Marketing Research, 41*(3), 293-305.

Richards, K. A., & Jones, E. (2008). Customer relationship management: finding value drivers. *Industrial Marketing Management, 37*(2), 120–130.

Customer Relationship Management (CRM) as a Function of Public Relations

Rodriguez, M., & Honeycutt, E. D. (2011). Customer Relationship Management (CRM)'s Impact on B to B Sales Professionals' Collaboration and Sales Performance. *Journal Of Business-To-Business Marketing, 18*(4), 335-356.

Rogers, E. M. (1962). *Diffusions of innovations*. New York: Free Press. (B2B CRM)

Rust, R.T., Inman, J., Jia, J., & Zahorik, A. (1999). What you don't know about customer-perceived quality: The role of customer expectation distribution. *Marketing Science, 18* (1), 77-92.

Ryals, L. (2005). Making customer relationship management work: The measurement and profitable management of customer relationships. *Journal of Marketing, 69*(4), 252-261.

Smith, N., Drumwright, M. E., & Gentile, M. C. (2010). The new marketing myopia. *Journal of Public Policy & Marketing, 29*(1), 4-11.

Sosa-Sosa, V., & Hernandez-Ramirez, E. M. (2012). A File Storage Service on a Cloud Computing Environment for Digital Libraries. *Information Technology & Libraries, 31*(4), 34-45.

Speier, C., & Venkatesh, V. (2002). The hidden minefields in the adoption of sales force automation technologies. *Journal of Marketing, 66*(3), 98-111.

Statistically speaking (2006). *CRM Magazine, 10*(8), 16.

Stoddard, J. (2009). Big Software, Little Price. *Journal of Financial Planning*, 6-7.

Sun, .B. (2006). Technology innovation and implications for customer relationship management. *Marketing Science, 25*(6), 594-597.

Tanner, J., Donthu, N., Gardner, M., Krishnamurthy, S., & Noble, S. (2005). Customer relationship management: A fad or a field?. *Journal of Marketing Research, 42*(2), 240 242.

Teven, J.J. & McCroskey, J.C., (1997). The relationship of perceived teacher caring with student learning and teacher evaluation. *Communication Education, 46*, 1-9.

Van Leuven, J. K., & Slater, M. D. (1991). How publics, public relations, and the media shape the public opinion process. *Public Relations Research Annual, 3*, 165-178.

Venkatesan, R., Kumar, V. V., & Bohling, T. (2007). Optimal customer relationship management using Bayesian decision theory: An application for customer selection. *Journal of Marketing Research, 44*(4), 579-594.

Wang, X., Dugan, R., & Sojka, J. (2013). CRM Systems with Social Networking Capabilities: The Value of Incorporating a CRM 2.0 System in Sales/Marketing Education. *Marketing Education Review, 23*(3), 241-250.

West, J. (2001). Customer relationship management and you. *IIE Solutions, 33*(4), 34.

Wise, K. (2007). Lobbying and relationship management: The K Street connection.

   Journal of Public Relations Research, 19(4), 357-376

Woodside, A. G., & Delozier, M. (1976). Effects of word of mouth advertising on consumer risk

   taking. *Journal of Advertising, 5*(4), 12-19.

Yim, C., Tse, D. K., & Chan, K. (2008). Strengthening customer loyalty through

   intimacy and passion: Roles of customer–firm affection and customer–staff relationships

   in services. *Journal of Marketing Research, 45*(6), 741-756.

Zablah, A. R., Bellenger, D. N.,&Johnston,W. J. (2004). An evaluation of divergent perspectives on

   customer relationship management: towards a common understanding of an emerging

   phenomenon. *Industrial Marketing Management, 33*(6), 475–489.

www.ingramcontent.com/pod-product-compliance
Lightning Source LLC
Chambersburg PA
CBHW041711200326
41518CB00001B/148